TWO CENTURIES OF ENGLISH CHINTZ
1750—1950

TWO CENTURIES OF ENGLISH CHINTZ 1750–1950

AS EXEMPLIFIED BY THE PRODUCTIONS OF STEAD, McALPIN & CO.

by

Cyril G. E. Bunt

and

Ernest A. Rose

THE

TEXTILE BOOK SERVICE
266 LAKE AVE. • P. O. BOX 178
METUCHEN, NEW JERSEY 08840

AND

PRINTED AND MADE IN ENGLAND

First published 1957

PRODUCED FOR AND UNDER THE SUPERVISION OF THE PUBLISHERS
AT THE DOLPHIN PRESS LTD., BRIGHTON.

CONTENTS

FOREWORD

IN PLANNING the present volume the authors have been actuated by a genuine enthusiasm for the art of the fabric printer and a desire to make more widely known the truly memorable example of business enterprise, whereby the old-established firm of Stead, McAlpin and Co., has consistently employed its well earned prestige to sustain and enhance the high standards of the whole industry.

In preparing the text they have been at pains to find a *via media* between the historical-technical, informative type of treatment, on the one hand, and one which might assume an aspect of stark advertisement on the other. Their ambition has been to present a book which, without being crowded with tedious details of processes, or over lavish praises of the Company's productions, will prove of interest to a wide range of readers.

As regards the variety and beauty of the Company's output the fine reproductions which have been carefully chosen as illustrations will speak for themselves. Every one has been photographed from the original printed fabric in the comprehensive collection preserved by the Company.

As we have said in the body of the text we look upon this venture as a species of exhibition, retrospective in part, with the advantage not possessed by an exhibition, of being permanently available for study, comparison and stimulation, to all who are interested in the subject of printed textiles.

G.C.E.B.
E.A.R.

1956

CHAPTER ONE

Early Events and the Wigton Stampery

PRIMARILY THE PURPOSE of this book is to provide for students of furnishing textile design a new and important series of examples, many of them unsurpassed in beauty and all masterpieces of British industry, illustrating the historic development of calico printing in England during the past two centuries. But it is the hope of both authors and publisher that it may prove of equal interest to the expert calico-printer and to the wider public upon whose taste and discrimination the industry depends for patronage. At the same time it is intended to serve as a tribute to one of the oldest and best-known firms of calico-printers in England—Messrs. Stead, McAlpin and Company Ltd., whose history is so intimately associated with the development of this fascinating form of decorative textile product throughout that period.

The making of Chintz—a term here employed to signify all printed cotton furnishing fabrics—is, and always has been since its first introduction, a peculiarly British industry and for centuries has been an index of the changing tastes of the domestic furnisher.

It has been said that Chintzes became popular because originally they supplied a peasant need; but calico-printing was never a peasant craft. The well-to-do draped their windows with brocaded silks and covered their chairs with needlepoint or tapestry. But, from at least the time of William and Mary, the only furnishing fabrics within the reach of the village upholsterer and middle-class urban populace was the printed calico or Chintz.

Nevertheless the craft was by no means of humble origin, for in the first instance the chintz makers aimed to provide a home-made substitute for the exotic and expensive printed and painted calicoes first brought into Europe by the Portuguese and Venetian merchant adventurers to the far-east.

This is not the occasion for entering into the history of calico-printing in India, so admirably done years ago by Collins-Baker. But we may recall a few interesting facts about its advent into Britain, so that we may obtain, in proper perspective, a picture of the industry's rise and progress.

We read that calico-printing was first brought to England by the Merchant Adventurers of the East India Company, but at least as early as 1592 an English privateer had brought into Devonport the Spanish carack *MADRE DE DIOS*, the cargo of which included calicoes, lawns, quilts, carpets and other rich commodities and it was this capture which decided the English merchants to establish direct communication with the Indies, resulting in the formation of the London East India Company, whose Charter was granted to them in the year 1600.

These captured calicoes (the name, of course, being a corruption of the place name Calicut, the Indian entrepôt) were in all probability specimens of the resplendent printed, painted or dyed fabrics and the quilts (the large hand-painted palampores) for which India was even then famed. From thence onwards, when the English Company was followed by the Dutch equivalent in 1602 and by the French Company in 1664, there was a steadily increasing demand for these oriental fabrics. But it was not until the seventies of the seventeenth century that the secrets of the Indian technique began to be acquired by Europeans.

As regards England, the late seventeenth century witnessed a gradually increasing flow of foreign craftsmen, Dutch and French, into the country, a flow which notably grew in volume during the last years of the century consequent upon the revocation of the Edict of Nantes in 1685.

The greater number of these migrants were silk weavers and textile printers, though gold and silversmiths, felt hat makers and other tradesmen were also included. In effect these craftsmen transplanted to the country of their adoption many of the well established industries of their native lands. They mostly settled first in and around the Metropolis, the silk-weavers at Spitalfields, the felt hat makers at Wandsworth, and the calico-printers at Richmond, Bow and Old Ford.

The first calico-printing factory in England is usually said to have been that at Richmond, or West Sheen as the village was then known. It was established by a Frenchman who came from Holland after the revocation of the Edict of Nantes. This may well have been the first considerable venture, but at least ten years before (in 1676) one William Sherwin, presumably an Englishman, had obtained 'A grant for fourteen years of the invention of a new and speedy way for producing broad cloth, which being the only true way of the East India printing and stayning such kind of goods'. It is not stated in what locality Sherwin operated, but the wording of the grant suggests that he was not alone in seeking to imitate the Indian 'Chint' makers. In 1690, the search for improved methods of imitating the Eastern originals was still going on, for in that year a Frenchman, Réné Grillet, likewise petitioned for a patent.

But the Richmond establishment (was Grillet, one wonders, the unnamed Frenchman responsible?) was the one which made history. The factory at West Sheen stood at a point hard by where the railway bridge now spans the river. The Old Deer Park now includes the spot where the village stood and the factory would seem to have occupied part of the site of the early fifteenth century Carthusian monastery where the celebrated Observatory was built later. Well into the eighteenth century there was a field close by known as the 'Bleaching Ground'.

A very considerable business was carried on here, numerous workpeople, both men and women, being employed who earned good wages and, it is said, were a 'saucy and independent lot'. It is related that, at the time, Richmond was over-run by calico-printers.

13

Dating from this seventeenth century, there is, in the British Museum collection, a rare trade-card of great interest, for it shows clearly the method by which chintzes were made at the time. It was issued by Jacob Stampe, a very appropriate name for one in the 'stampery' trade. It announces that 'Jacob Stampe living at ye sighn of the Callico Printer in the Hounsditch Prints all sorts of Callicoe Linings Silkes Stuffs New and Ould at Reasonable Rates'. Its pictorial element, a rough woodcut, shows a craftsman printer at work at a table upon which is spread out a length of cloth, falling in folds on to the floor. In one hand he grasps a wooden block which he is applying to the material, in the other he holds the maul, used to strike the block and so imprint the pattern in its appropriate place. Behind him stands the tierer with a tub of colour, ready to supply the master man anew before each repeat.

While these and other 'stamperies' were establishing the industry on English soil, the imported Indian printed calicoes reached a pitch of popularity among those who could afford them at which the wool and silk industries grew concerned. So much so that, at the turn of the century, they obtained from Parliament the prohibition of all such oriental goods. This had the result, which might well have been anticipated, of boosting the new industry of the English calico-printers and, in 1720, the ban was extended to include these—a fact which speaks eloquently of the wide popularity of the English products. If we were in any doubt, the following extracts from 'The Spittlefields Ballads or the Weaver's Complaint against the Callico Madams' would convince us:—

> Our trade is so bad
> That the weavers run mad
> Through the want of both work and provisions,
> That some hungry poor rogues
> Feed on grains like our hogs,
> They're reduced to such wretched conditions.

14

Then well may they tayre
What our ladies now wear
And as foes to our country upbraid 'em,
Till none shall be thought
A more scandalous slut
Than a tawdry Callico Madam.

When our trade was in wealth
Our women had health,
We'd silks, rich embroideries and satins,
Fine stuffs and good crapes
For each ord'nary trapes
That is destin'd to hobble in pattens;
But now we've a Chince
For the wife of a prince,
And a butterfly gown for a gay dame,
Thin painted old sheets
For each trull in the streets
To appear like a Callico Madam.

There is much more in a similar strain and the ballad maker
even turns his wrath upon those males who countenanced
the wearing of chintzes.

. . . .

Its no matter at all
If the Prince of Iniquity had 'em,
Or that each for a bride
Should be cursedly tied
To some damn'd Callico Madam.

On one occasion this riot of the weavers became so violent
that they tore the offending garments from the backs of the
women in the streets. It was shortly after this that, as we have
already said, the ban was placed upon English chintzes. The
Gentleman's Magazine for 1768 records that as late as that, two
women were fined £5 by the Lord Mayor for wearing chintz
gowns.

Despite all opposition, the industry survived. While the continued importation of Indian calicoes was forced 'underground', the English calico-printers to some extent circumvented the prohibition by the use of a mixed fabric of silk and cotton. Cotton printing in one colour only was never affected. The restriction was not finally lifted until 1774, after the famous Arkwright had, by his inventions, made possible a satisfactory all-cotton English calico.

Even before 1700, Bromley-by-Bow, on the river Lee, was a calico-printing centre, the largest of all the early print works being the famous Bromley Hall, first mentioned in the seventeen-forties, the productions of which are to be estimated by the Bromley Hall Pattern Book, now preserved at the Victoria and Albert Museum. These are paper impressions from copper-plate designs, 141 in number, which reminds us that as early as 1752 the use of copper-plates was competing with the more ancient wood-block technique. Francis Nixon and T. Thompson employed copper plates at Drumcondra, near Dublin, before the former came over to settle at Phipp's Bridge, Merton, where John Nixon his son, continued until 1789. Contemporary with this, there was the establishment of Robert Jones at Old Ford, which closed in 1780. At the sale of his equipment there were 200 copper plates and 2,000 blocks and prints, showing clearly that the older form of printing was by no means superceded by the newer process. Writing of this eighteenth century output, Jean Ryhiner, of Basle, himself a cotton-printer, tells us in 1766 that the elegance of their designs and the beauty of their printing surpassed all their rivals.

We cannot here chronicle all the steps by which the art of calico-printing as a British industry progressed towards complete success, for all we have recounted merely brings us to the threshold of our period. But an important point to be mentioned here is that the art was first practised in Scotland in 1738, a quarter of a century before its introduction into Lan-

16

cashire. The printing of silks was well established long before that, of course; but however tentative the industry of cotton-printing may have been north of the Tweed in its earlier days, this fact assumes importance when we learn that some years later, about the time when Bonnie Prince Charlie came over the Border in 1745, Kenneth McAlpin likewise came down into England and settled in Wigton, in Cumberland. Here, according to one account, he established a small dye-works. It is not known whether Kenneth McAlpin actually came south in the train of the Young Pretender or not. He may have done so and then have settled in Wigton after Culloden. However this may have been, we may surmise that he had already learned the craft in Scotland, since, if the story be true, he could hardly have founded even a small dye works without previous experience.

All things considered, however, it would seem most probable that he first found employment with an existing concern. Wigton's name was already coupled with the production of tow cloth, Osnaberghs, heavy bleached linens and striped checks. But, more to the point, there was what the *Carlisle Patriot* in 1845 called the 'Old established calico-printing works' of Messrs: Halliley and Co. at Burnfoot, Wigton, which had been established about the middle of the eighteenth century. These works were known as 'The Stampery' and, in the following century, as the 'Old Printworks' until they were burnt down in 1845.

From all the evidence we have been able to gather—all too little we must admit—it is at least probable that the original Kenneth McAlpin may have been connected with this establishment, for it is elsewhere on record that one Thomas McAlpin, a direct descendant of Kenneth, had a son Nathan, who is referred to as the 'Manager of a print-works at Wigton called the Stampery'.

Here, then, we have the beginnings from which later grew into being the since famous firm of Stead, McAlpin and Co.,

17

which for close on two centuries has been identified with all that is best in the calico-printing industry. Today it is one of the four largest and oldest textile concerns in the country.

We have no means of telling to how great an extent the productions of this Wigton 'Stampery' contributed to the successes which earned the industrious 1760's the reputation of being the golden period of chintz printing. It was a far cry from Wigton to London, which was always the centre of production, where Robert Jones of Old Ford, the Ollives, Talwins and Fosters of Bromley Hall and the two Nixons of Phipp's Bridge, Merton, set a standard of high excellence. But the Wigton works must have grown and their success must have bred emulation for, in 1790, another manufactory of printed calicoes was established at Spittal, about a quarter of a mile from the town by Messrs. Bromwell and Irving.

Of these London factories it should be noted that Old Ford closed down in 1780 and Phipp's Bridge, Merton, in 1789. It is on record that between 1790 and 1810 many thousands of old copper plates, as well as wood-blocks, were sold on the closing of most of the old-established London firms. Though we have mentioned only two of the many these two were quite important concerns and their closing indicates the fact that, towards the close of the eighteenth century, London lost its supremacy to the growing number of factories which had begun to operate in the north.

The great manufacturing towns, such as Manchester, were increasing in importance and Lancashire was laying the foundations of its important cotton trade. It was, therefore, no wonder that the textile-printing industry assumed, almost suddenly, a new orientation focussed upon the industrial north; and that, as the great firms of the south dropped out of the running, their place was taken in the home market by these northerners and given a new lease of life.

Great changes were in the offing, or to change the metaphor the birth of the machine age was imminent. For the textile-printing industry an important event was the invention by Thomas Bell of printing by cylinders, patented in 1783. While hitherto the older wood-block method was one of stamping, the copper-engraved plates had been printed on flat-bed presses—just as the engraved prints on paper were produced. It need hardly be said that a method of printing from engraved rotary cylinders was a revolutionary step forward—an industrial revolution in more ways than one when it became generally adopted.

As regards the patterns, the earliest surviving pattern-books, which only came to light at the time of the Cotton Board Exhibition of 1955, proving a revelation to all who saw them, show but one colour, since they were no more than impressions, taken for record purposes. All the early calicoes were printed by the laborious 'Madder Style' as it has been termed, and were virtually monochromes. Reds, lilacs and blacks were produced by alum and iron mordants, madder dyed; the yellows and drabs by weld or quercitron dyeing, the blues being put in with the brush. But revolution was soon to come. By the end of the century wood-blocks printed in two colour ranges—in the drabs and greens from quercitron bark and indigo—were already predominent and, from about 1800, polychrome wood-block prints were in production in the full range of colours resulting from madder, quercitron and indigo. The catalogue of the Exhibition held under the auspices of the Cotton Board gives us an idea of the variety of patterns so produced. More will be said upon this aspect of the question in later pages.

It has been deemed necessary to refer to these details incident to this period of transition because at this important juncture, although we have no precise information about the McAlpin print works at Wigton, we may be sure that they moved with the times and kept abreast of all the latest technique. That they prospered is quite certain and there is sufficient evidence to show that at the turn of the century, their dyeing

19

industry had made satisfactory progress and, in addition certain types of simple printing by block and discharge methods had been successfully mastered. It is safe therefore to assume that, since a dyeing process was fundamentally the basis—either resist or discharge—the original dye works was entirely merged in the calico-printing works known as The Stampery.

As time went on and development took place it began to be realised that these works, by now quite firmly established at Wigton, would not much longer be adequate to meet their progressive needs. Besides which, as public demand increased, other companies were springing up elsewhere, which, while spurring them on by competition, assured them of further progress in the future.

It was not until 1835, however that any radical change was effected. It came about in the following way. One of the newer competing companies referred to above was at Cummersdale, Carlisle. This Cummersdale Print Works, as it was called, was about twelve miles to the north of Wigton. It was apparently built and financed by a Mr. John Forster a banker of Carlisle, who established the business of calico printing here under the name of Forster, James and Co., (afterwards to become Forster, James, Wastell, Donald and Co.) under the last mentioned as Manager. For a few years this venture was successful and, indeed became a keen rival of McAlpin of Wigton. 'The garment prints produced here were in great request and considered second to none at the time for good workmanship and fastness of colour' according to Whellam's *History of Cumberland* of 1860. Despite this the firm failed in the year 1817 and the works remained totally unoccupied for seventeen years.

Thus in 1835 the derelict premises which were in a sadly delapidated condition were purchased by Thomas McAlpin and Co. Some time before this Thomas McAlpin had married the widow of a Mr. Stead, head of a coal mining company at Bolton-Low-Houses, near Wigton, and his step-son John Stead, a young man of twenty-six, came into the business.

For the Cummersdale works, so long unoccupied and ruinous that the records speak of it as 'this wreck of a place' the price paid was £4,000. It included a dwelling house, several workers' cottages and four acres of land. Under its new ownership it was reconditioned without delay, so that it was operating the very same year, equipped with up-to-date plant, with the main power derived from a large water-wheel.

By then the Company had quite outgrown the capacity of the old works at Wigton and the whole concern, 'lock, stock and barrel' was transferred to the new premises, together with most, if not all,of the personnel. We should remember that this was some years before the railways were extended to this part of the world which event took place in 1842, so the exodus was carried out by road, the work people on foot wheeling their possessions the whole twelve miles in hand carts and barrows. We reproduce the photograph of a charcoal drawing purporting to depict one aspect of this memorable migration. Though entirely imaginary, we feel that it is of interest, its

piquant humour portraying an incident that might well have had its counterpart on that memorable occasion—except that to the best of our knowledge no rotary machine had ever found place in the Wigton factory.

We have already recorded that the works at Wigton were known as The Stampery, a term which clearly conveys the information that, from the first, the firm was identified with the original wood-block process, which has ever continued to be their speciality. Unfortunately, perhaps, the expressive name was never officially used by the Company at Cummersdale and in time ceased to be familiar. But the old name was, to some extent, bound to be transferred if only as a generic description and persisted among the 'old hands' who had been so long associated with Wigton. Indeed the name must have been perpetuated well into the next generation, for many of the older employees of today can well remember their parents referring to the Cummersdale works under the old name.

An interesting survival having reference to the original Cummersdale premises may perhaps be mentioned here. A part of the old buildings yet remaining is still spoken of as the 'Convict Shop' by some of the older employees. In the early days such organisations as Trade Unions were unheard of. But there existed among these early nineteenth century craftsmen a real sense of responsibility to their employers and themselves, as well as a pride in the quality of the work they were helping to produce. Any workman who 'let the side down' by doing bad work was penalized by some sort of fine and was transferred to the 'Convict Shop' as a punishment. Another part of the original building still in use is known popularly as 'The Chapel'. Though it is now only used for storage purposes, it was doubtless at one time used as a place of worship.

CHAPTER TWO

Developments at Cummersdale

THE CALICO-PRINTING INDUSTRY was established in Carlisle in 1761 and before the close of the century had grown to be the principal local industry with four firms actively employing a thousand hands between them. We are not surprised, therefore, to find in the early years of the nineteenth century the City already ranked as an important centre in the development of the textile manufacture, both in weaving and printing. The City's records reveal that thousands of women and children were employed in the 'Printing Fields', in and around the neighbourhood, mostly adjacent to the stream, the waters of which the earlier pioneers had discovered to possess certain qualities which were essential, or at least desirable, in the preparation of the finished product as it passed through the bleaching and dyeing processes.

These 'Printing Fields' were then a very necessary part of the industry, since one of the difficulties in the early evolution of calico-printing in this country was to impart to the woven piece goods that degree of whiteness so essential if the colours, whether printed or dyed, were to result in a rich and brilliant effect. We are all familiar with the pronounced difference between bleached and unbleached calico and at the period in question there were no known chemical bleaching agents such as chemistry provides today; nor had the English producer the powerful aid which a tropical sun provided in India. So the woven calico, after washing and scouring to get rid of all impurities, was spread upon the grassy fields to allow the atmosphere, the wind and the rain and such sun as nature vouchsafed, to effect the necessary bleaching. Hence, no doubt, the employment of so many women and children, whose task consisted in turning, pegging down and otherwise manipulating the lengths of cloth—a continuous task whatever the weather.

23

Only when thoroughly bleached were they ready for the skilled attention of the printer.

At this comparatively early period most of the printing was done, as we have explained, by the hand-block method, the principles of which were originally derived from the East, chiefly from India, where with the most primitive equipment the caste of Dyers had developed the art of creating with their vegetable colours their remarkable chintzes and stained or painted palampores. Although it seems certain that they had no assistance from any 'designers' as we now understand the term, yet the traditional use and blending of their vegetable dyes to produce the significant patterns, handed down from generation to generation, resulted in satisfying qualities of beauty. These very patterns provided a compendium of inspiration for the early block-printed patterns of the West. To what extent this influence was reflected in our English chintzes may be seen in examples spoken of in a later chapter.

It was into an environment of comparatively primitive methods that the firm of Thomas McAlpin moved when Cummersdale works were acquired in 1835. The success achieved at Wigton had accrued from the perhaps exclusive use of the block-printing technique. We have no evidence that the engraved copper-plate method was employed there, though as we have seen, this technique had been exploited to the full by the calico-printers in and around London. But half a century before the acquisition of Cummersdale the Scotsman Thomas Bell had (in 1783) invented the method of printing by rotary metal cylinders, which was destined to supercede to some extent the older techniques. Other epoch-making events had also taken place, the discovery of new dyestuffs, of new mineral colours, new chemical resists and discharges, so that the newly named firm of McAlpin, Stead and Co. had, in this move to the neighbourhood of Carlisle, opportunity to avail themselves of 'all the latest improvements'.

The first machines were installed at Cummersdale in 1835. But, as they only printed in two or three colours the range was restricted and the innovation did not in any way seriously interfere with their earlier reputation for block-printed textiles. At the time it was no doubt thought that the newer and more speedy roller-printing would supplant the older and slower method. But as time went on it was realized that there was to be a steady demand for the products of both methods.

During the early Victorian era there took place rapid development in the employment of machine printing and the Company's records show that a number of new machines for printing from engraved copper rollers were introduced, together with all the necessary subsidiary plant required for the preparatory and finishing processes. It was about this time that the printed cotton roller blind, first introduced round about 1825, became universally popular and to facilitate output (since the block-print method proved to be too slow) the Company installed a duplex printing machine (printing on both sides of the material, which thus became reversable) to print widths up to 60 inches. For this they obtained a patent. It may be said that this portion of their output proved to be of great importance and, as the demand for machine-printed fabrics of all kinds increased, serious attention had to be devoted to the question of the engraving of the copper rollers, a matter which played an important rôle in the quality and effect of the goods produced.

The result was that the Company installed a plant to enable them to do their own engraving and, by a system of apprenticeship, they gradually built up a team of first-class craftsmen in this highly skilled task of transferring designs from the artist's drawings to the rollers. As time went on it became abundantly apparent that, by their skill and enterprise, the Cummersdale engravers had set up a standard of workmanship which was second to none in this rapidly developing side of the industry. It became in time one of the Company's chief assets in the bid for patronage, in which at the time they had to meet keen competition, not only from producers in the home market, but also in France and Germany.

Despite such developments in mechanical production and the fears which had been felt of their effect upon the continued use of the old block-printing method, the latter, though for a time it suffered a severe set-back, soon recovered. The revival was doubtless due to a renewed demand for those beautiful floral designs which (themselves inspired by the floral patterns of the late eighteenth century) were first brought to popular notice at the Great Exhibition in Hyde Park, London, in 1851, and repeated ten years later at the International Exhibition of 1862. At the latter, Stead, McAlpin and Co. were awarded Gold Medals for their block-printed exhibits and this stimulated the already wide demand for these beautiful English floral designs resulting in the creation of a widespread vogue for flowering chintzes for all types of household furnishing fabrics.

In the early eighteen-fifties Thomas McAlpin died and John Stead became sole proprietor. The name of the Company was then changed to Stead, McAlpin and Co. and under the *aegis* of this now famous name, since identified with all that is best in calico-printing, it earned an ever increasing reputation. There were other firms of course, of equal rank—the Calico Printers' Association of Manchester, Messrs. G. P. and J. Baker of Crayford and Messrs. Turnbull and Stockdale of Ramsbottom—but Stead, McAlpin and Co. were renowned as specialists in block-printing.

After the Franco-Prussian War of 1870-71, when a big demand arose for English printed fabrics, the Company, to meet the contingency, installed multi-coloured printing machines, and, since it was about this time that the development of coal-tar colours was in process of revolutionizing the dyeing industry, it was not long before both 30 inch and 50 inch fabrics were being printed in any number of colours from six to sixteen. This rapid and dual development in both mechanization and colour range was responsible for once more giving rise to doubts in the block-printers' minds as to whether the old method could possibly survive and compete with the mechanically produced materials. But once again such fears were proved to be without foundation. The demand created in the fifties did not die out and, despite keen competition with other Companies in this Country, to say nothing of those of France and Germany, the enterprise and *esprit de corps* of the Cummersdale factory easily held its own.

So much faith had they in the future of this branch of their activities that in 1893 they purchased the very valuable collection of hand blocks of the famous Bannister Hall Print Works, near Preston, Lancashire. This collection has rightly been described as unique for it comprises about 3,800 documented cloth samples of wood-block prints dating from 1802 to 1840, as well as some 900 designs dating from 1799 to 1804. A few years later the Summerseat Print Works was absorbed and the valuable collection of blocks and other plant was transferred to Cummersdale, together with many of the printers. These facts will serve to show that Stead, McAlpin and Co. had faith in their own judgment in this matter of the future of block-printed fabrics.

For close upon forty years, until his death in 1891, John Stead, with the assistance from 1880 of his son, Edmund Wright Stead, carried the Company along in its prosperous career, the son continuing in the direction after his father until 1934, having turned it into a private Limited Company ten years earlier. Edmund Wright Stead steered the concern through the seriously difficult times of the first Great War of 1914-18 and guided it back to the revival which was soon under way. He was responsible for one of Cummersdale's most important developments of later years, for he installed the plant for the process known as Surface Printing by wooden rollers. The principles of this method were not entirely new to the industry, having been already used in a primitive form by colour-printers, and had already been employed in the printing of wall-papers. France had given the lead in its application to textiles. But as developed it was an epoch-making advance in technique.

It was, of course, a rotary process which was operated in much the same way as that previously in use with engraved rollers. But the method of applying the colours was directly opposite to that of the engraved cylinders. The rollers were made with well seasoned, hard-wood centres encased in sheathing of softer wood (usually Sycamore). Upon this the design was cut, one roller being required for each colour desired. The design was cut upon each in much the same way as it had been on the hand-blocks, but obviously making allowances for the cylindrical surfaces. In short the colours were applied by printing from the surface, whereas, in the engraved-copper process the colour was taken up by the cloth from the engraved lines cut into the metal. We give illustrations which demonstrate the principle (fig. 1).

At Cummersdale the work of cutting the rollers for this surface-printing technique was of course carried out by the same craftsmen who cut the hand-blocks, the works was there-fore well equipped for the production of this type of work and, as in the cases of its enterprise in the art of copper-roller engraving, this resulted before very long in the training of a team of expert craftsmen, well able to cut the necessary volume of wooden rollers required to meet the growing demand for this type of printed work. But, like all hand-work, it took many weeks to cut even one set of sixteen rollers, a fact better to be appreciated when we consider that a full set of cutters' tools numbered not less than a hundred, each having to be selected and utilised with a trained hand and eye. When once cut, such a set of rollers would last for many years and could be varied as often as deemed desirable by alteration of the colour schemes.

The time taken in the production of block-printed fabrics has always been a difficulty in their economic manufacture, and although of recent years improved methods have been introduced in an endeavour to speed up production in this department, it has to be acknowledged that, if they are to retain that artistic charm and simple beauty for which hand-block printed fabrics have ever been renowned, very little can be done to improve the time factor in their production.

We should endeavour to vizualise that a first class block-printer and his mate have to work very industriously to print one piece of an average block design in a week and then many further processes have to be gone through, and if he is printing from one of the original old blocks he may, because of their colour-shading, find they have to be printed by what is known as the Two Course principle, which means that some of the colours have to be printed first, then developed, washed and dried and then returned to the table for the remaining colours to be put in, thus materially adding to the time taken. Yet this extra time expended is absolutely essential to complete success, for in many cases the second course colours over-print those of the first course and only by this method can be achieved that subtle shaded effect which was so justly esteemed in the old days and which still stands in high regard among high grade decorators of today (fig. 2).

In the early nineteen-twenties the whole calico-printing industry began to realize that, if the use of printed fabrics for furnishing and dress materials was to retain its popularity, a type of colour quality must be achieved which would appeal to a much wider section of the general public. About this time, too, a new range of colours was perfected for dyeing purposes which gave a much higher degree of fastness against light and washing. The Cummersdale Company very soon realized that if this new range of colours could be made use of in printing it would be a great boon to the industry in general, since it would mean that for the first time it would be possible to produce printed fabrics with guaranteed reasonably fast colours.

The application of this range of vat colours to the requirements of the industry involved a great deal of new plant being installed—not so much for the actual printing as for various new methods in the preparation and finishing. The requisite plant having been installed Cummersdale soon became the centre of many experiments which were destined to revolutionize the older technique of machine printing and to put upon the market a range of designs, all printed with vat colours, which in a very short time achieved a great success.

Edmund Wright Stead, as Governing Director of the private Limited Company, as it had been since 1924, was known to all his staff as 'E.W.S.'. He was a great personality and a born leader. The well-being of his employees was one of his constant concerns. He knew them all young and old, high and low, and earned their devotion by his lively interest in their fortunes, especially with regard to those who through sickness or advancing years were unable to continue their work and perforce had to be taken off the Company's pay-roll. Such persons were never removed from his personal pay-roll until such time as he was assured of their comfort and well-being. This, of course, was before the time when a Welfare State and National Pension schemes removed the necessity for such individual benevolence and the personal interest he, as the chief, thus evinced in the lives of those who had worked for him was invaluable in creating an atmosphere of trust and devotion which, one may say, paid its own dividends in material integrity, the like of which could never result from the impersonal benefits conferred by legislation.

The next important development in the history of textile printing took place in the early thirties of the present century with the introduction of Screen Printing. In this as in other developments the Company again was one of the Pioneers.

The principle involved was made possible by the development of photography, the screen itself being a wooden frame on which was stretched a fine copper or silk gauze. This was prepared with a solution which, acting as a stencil, allowed the features of the design to be applied to the cloth through the gauze by rollers, each colour requiring a separate screen. A given design might consist of any number of colours, from one to sixteen (twenty in exceptional cases) and one of the main factors to be considered was how to produce the desired effect by the use of a minimum number of screens, thus keeping production costs as low as possible.

In its early stages of development the actual printing was all done by hand on short, twelve yard long tables, such as had previously been used for block-printing. But as time went on it was found that this method was too slow to allow demands to be met. The Company therefore decided to build a new shop to accommodate printing tables of a length to take full piece-lengths of sixty to seventy yards. These full-length tables enabled the printers to complete each piece without the disadvantage of having to move the cloth at the completion of each twelve yards. This however was only one of the advantages gained by this new method of printing from the screens. Experience in the working of this process began to show how improved technical and mechanical adjustments could be applied both to the making of the screens and the details of printing, thus enabling the attainment of greater efficiency and the saving of time, all so essential in the keen competition for the world's markets (figs. 3 and 4).

The success of this new venture soon became apparent and a further new shop was added, doubling the output capacity and today the Company possesses one of the finest screen-printing plants in the country. Since 1945 moreover a considerable amount of other new plant has been installed, which has enabled Cummersdale to keep pace with modern requirements. New buildings have been erected, new boilers have been installed, colour houses and laboratories have been renewed, a new Ager, so essential for the developing and fixing of the fast vat colour ranges, an air-lay drier for finishing of linens and unions, all have helped materially towards making Cummersdale one of the most up-to-date and comprehensive textile printing works (fig. 5).

When electricity became an important commercial proposition for power and light Cummersdale installed its own generating plant for both. Moreover, it produced the necessary current to light the houses and cottages in the two villages of Upper and Lower Cummersdale. Although the lighting and power in the villages have in recent years been taken over by the local Council, the works still continues to generate the whole of its power and lighting.

But despite all these developments and widening of their interests the Company has never lost sight of the importance and the distinction gained by a century and a half of specialising in block-printed fabrics. Always their blocks have been carefully preserved and it is safe to say that the collection possessed by Cummersdale today is probably the finest in the world. It comprises representative designs of all periods, collected over generations, which must be unique in the history of the calico printing industry.

Many writers of the nineteenth century, when speaking of the English hand-block productions express the view that the chintzes of the 'William and Mary' and early Georgian styles were possibly, both in design and colour, the most beautiful of all time. Whether this is so or not, it can be truly said that these periods were responsible for the nurture of the printed textile arts. The productions of these early days very soon achieved a fame equal to that of the silks and brocades as decorations in the stately homes of the English aristocracy.

The beauty of these printed fabrics, with their delicate drawing and gay colouring, their floral bouquets, their exotic birds and other brilliant conceits found fame even on the Continent, and although their exportation was forbidden at the time, many examples found their way to France, Germany

32

and Russia. Today examples are to be seen in many Continental Museums.

It was after this golden period, of course, that the rapid development of machine printing revolutionised the industry. But, as we know, time has shown that there is a good and expanding market for the productions by both hand-block and machine. Thus we see how wise was the policy of the Company to preserve their fine collection of blocks and, in fact, to add to them as we have already said.

During the last few years a general shortage of man power and ever increasing competition has resulted in great efforts being made to raise productivity by the introduction of new methods. It is not surprising, therefore, that with their usual foresight and energy the Management began to interest themselves in the experiments in what was known as 'Time and Motion Studies', later to be generalized under the name 'Automation'.

As often happens in factories with generations of traditional practice behind them, the workers at Cummersdale viewed with some apprehension the first suggestions of the Management to bring in more modern methods of working. It was, in fact, sometime before a general agreement was reached to try out various 'time studies' which aimed at increased productivity while reducing effort, thus making it possible to increase earnings without any increase in expended energy. These efforts were successful, so much so that they earned publicity in the pages of *Target*—a publication sponsored by the Central Office of Information, to encourage industrial development and publicise methods by which 'Automation' could increase production. In an issue of *Target* in 1952 Cummersdale was quoted, showing a new type of core for copper-roller fabric printing which has been adopted and not only saves considerable time and labour in assembling, but also improves the quality of the printing (see also p. 75).

Among other improvements resulting from 'Motion Study' at the works perhaps the most important is one in the

33

field of hand-block printing. The technique has always called for craftsmanship of a high order and the traditional mode of procedure, was, until comparatively recently, considered to be incapable of improvement. For generations the tierer's trolley was a heavy contraption running on rails side by side with the table and every time the printer wished to recharge his block with colour he had to turn away from the table to do so, carrying his block with him. Now this heavy type of trolley has been replaced by a light tubular structure with an aluminium tray extending over and across the table, so that the printer has no need to turn away. Moreover, in the case of large hand-blocks, some of which weigh as much as twenty pounds, the block is now suspended on strong elastic cords, so that its weight is supported from above on a movable pulley-arm fixed to the trolley. Both these improvements result in a very considerable saving of time and energy and increase productivity by as much as twenty per cent (figs. 6 and 7).

CHAPTER THREE

American contacts, an exhibition and the question of design

BY THE MIDDLE of the nineteenth century England was entirely committed to dependence upon the railways for the development of its industries. Inevitably, therefore, although as we have already recorded the great group of textile industries was concentrated in the northern counties, yet the directive in the Provinces could never function to full satisfaction without that contact which only a London office could make with the home and overseas markets under such conditions. London as the Metropolis and paramount nerve-centre of most industrial enterprises has therefore been for over a century the focal point for sales and distribution in the textile world, the Cheapside and Wood Street areas of the City being the localities where its merchants foregathered. It is therefore not surprising to find from the old records of the Company that over a century ago Stead, McAlpin and Co. had established offices and show-rooms in the midst of this area, first in Bread Street and later in Gresham Street. The latter served the purposes of the Company until the first World War, when it was found that larger premises were desirable to cope with the ever expanding volume of sales. A move was therefore made to much more extensive premises in Warwick Lane, which thus became the centre of its activities until, at the close of 1941, the whole building with its valuable contents and records was totally destroyed in the great City fire. In spite of this disastrous loss, temporary offices were soon established in Holborn. But again, a year later, these were in their turn destroyed by enemy action. A move was then made to the West End where offices were opened in Regent Street. However, in 1946 it was decided that a return to the City was desirable. So new offices and showrooms were established in

Greenwich House, Newgate Street, which have ever since remained the headquarters of the Company.

In addition to offices in London the firm has from time to time maintained an office in Manchester, but London has always remained the chief centre, not only for sales, but as a focal point for the meeting of artists and the interviewing of overseas buyers, particularly our many friends from the United States, who, as we have pointed out, have been our best customers for hand-block printed productions. Most of these find it worth while to make annual visits to Europe in the interests of their many customers and invariably find a cordial welcome at Greenwich House.

On the Company's side these friendly visits are reciprocated by periodic trips to the States. For many years Mr. Rose, co-author of the present book, made an annual visit to the United States on their behalf.

'Perhaps one of the most vivid memories I have,' he records, 'was of the trip I made to New York in the early days of the second World War. It will be remembered that furnishing fabrics as such had been declared non-essential. All national efforts were centred upon the conduct of the war and certain of our engineering sections were turned over to war-work. But we still had our hand-block section, which was a potential dollar earner, if only the necessary orders could be secured. And, as the United States (who had not then entered the conflict) was the only possible market, it was decided, in co-operation with the Board of Trade, that I should make the journey.

'I left for Liverpool at the end of September 1941, not knowing by what ship I was to cross the Atlantic. But after a few days I was allocated a cabin on a famous Cunard liner and eventually arrived at New York towards the middle of October, receiving a hearty welcome from my many American friends. Fortunately the support I received in the way of orders fully justified the journey under trying conditions and much valuable business was secured, which not only benefited Cummersdale by helping to keep together its craftsmen in the block-printing shops, but the many shipments of goods which continued to cross the Atlantic during the ensuing years were of material value to the country's economy.

'Having completed my mission by the early part of December, I hoped to get back home by Christmas. To my great disappointment, however, I was soon to learn that there was little or no hope of obtaining a passage in the foreseeable future, owing to enemy activity in the Atlantic. It was not until April 1942, in fact, that I was finally allowed (thanks to the influence of the British Consul) to fly by an American Clipper to Lisbon via Bermuda and the Azores, there to await a plane home. The journey occupied eigtht days from the time of leaving New York. Some months later my trunks of samples and personal luggage which I was of course unable to bring with me, were shipped by our agents direct to Liverpool and, although they reached the quayside safely, they were all destroyed by fire through enemy action. This was the final episode in a chain of circumstances marking the visit planned to last six weeks which in fact took six months.'

The severely restricted era of the second World War was eventually survived and, like the whole industrial life of the country, the textile printing industry faced the problems of recovery incident to the early post-war period. But with the year 1949 came one of the proudest moments in the long history of Stead, McAlpin and Co. In that year, at the invitation of the Cotton Board, they organized and presented an exhibition of printed furnishing fabrics at the Style and Design Centre of the Board in Manchester.

During the years immediately succeeding the war it became obvious to all in the textile trade that a new directive, a new stimulus, was urgently needed if Britain was to regain and hold the proud position she had reached in pre-war days. Some fresh incentive was especially necessary in the all-important realms of design and its application to printed fabrics.

The Central organization of the Cotton Board had therefore resolved to give all the assistance in its power in an endeavour to increase and expand the production of this staple British industry. Hence their sponsorship of this exhibition. Not only had the home consumers lived through a severely rationed period of 'make do and mend', with utility as the operative idea in the production of all piece goods, but even the export markets, so necessary to the economic life of the country, had been very seriously impaired by the limitations placed on output.

This exhibition was therefore planned to be a 'shop window for the trade' and was devised with the object of stimulating interest in the achievements of the past, while at the same time inculcating a spirit of courageous emulation in the minds of a new generation of producers. Thus, while in a way it was intended to accentuate the high standards, both in design and execution, which this important branch of British industry had achieved, it aimed at the same time at inspiring a new spirit of adventurous planning for the future.

The organizers therefore kept in mind as a chief objective the assembly of a display which would show the many developments which had taken place in the furnishing fabric industry from the early days up to modern times, illustrating with actual fabrics both the methods of production and the evolution of taste in design. It was frankly hoped (and the hope was fully justified by the subsequent results) that it would prove of especial value by providing an opportunity for many of the younger generation (who were entering the industry after war service) to gain an insight into what this important section of the textile trade had accomplished.

Not the least interesting feature of the show was the revolutionary method of display adopted. It had been designed and carried out by the Nicholson brothers, who at the time were among the best known of modern display artists. Our fig. 8, showing just one corner of the Exhibition Hall, will give some idea of the essentially modern spirit in which the whole was carried out and how appropriately it might have been termed, as we have suggested, a Shop Window for the Trade.

The method of display did full justice to the exhibits, suggestive, as they needed to be, of the gravitational pliancy of the soft cotton materials as used in various decorative contingencies. The opening ceremony was officially performed by Sir Raymond Streat, the Chairman of the Cotton Board, and during the three weeks it remained open to the public was visited by many thousands of representatives of the trade as well as the general public. So far as the objective of the organizers was concerned, one of the most gratifying features was the very large number of young students and artists who signed the visitors' book. From their demeanour and appreciative remarks which were expressed on many occasions it was evident that they derived a great deal of pleasure and no small amount of edification from this representative display of beautiful printed fabrics. It is safe to assume that this young generation had never before had the opportunity of studying so unique a display and of thus becoming *au fait* with the more modern trends and developments which they then viewed in their true perspective.

Among the many important visitors we must certainly include 'The American Maid of Cotton' who, with her official associates, honoured the exhibition with a visit of ceremony during her tour of this country. She represented an American organization which had sponsored a transatlantic movement to boost 'Cotton' and its importance in its relation to fashion in fabrics. We reproduce a photograph (fig. 9) which shows this 'Maid' admiring the block-printed design 'Old Chelsea' (which is the subject of our fig. 39) and other historic block-printed chintzes.

The exhibition, for the all-too-brief period that it remained open, served much the same purpose which we are attempting to achieve in a more permanent way by the publication of the present series of reproductions. Since in both the accent is, as it should be, on Design, it would seem appropriate that we should here devote a few words to showing the importance the Company has always attached to good design.

There is considerable evidence to show that even in its very early days the establishment had its own studios and employed a number of artists who worked in close co-operation with the skilled operatives. In fact the Company's successful achievements give us every reason to believe that these artists, in preparing their drawings, were not only concerned with artistic qualities, but also with the vital question of their practical transference from the drawing-board to the printed fabrics. It was this close co-operation between the designer and the technician which secured satisfactory results in all important matters such as scale and size in relation to width, etc. Above all, perhaps, it took cognizance of the possibility of rendering the colours chosen by the means available to the printers. This desirable state of affairs would seem to have continued with excellent results well into the Victorian era.

But in the eighteen-seventies there came about a revolutionary change. The great artist-craftsman, William Morris, by his genius and enterprise in many phases of creative art reoriented the relationship between art and industry. His teachings and practical example had profound repercussions throughout the realms of art and were given still further impetus through the Arts and Crafts Movement which was founded in 1883 with the formation of the Arts and Crafts Exhibition Society. From this time onwards the monopoly of the professional textile designer gave place to the artist-designer, the commercial or free-lance artist who, so far as our industry was concerned, would seem to have anticipated the immense possibilities that the designing of textiles was to provide.

Trained to design in a wider field than those professionally attached to the industry, they naturally developed more personal, individual styles, to a great extent non-traditional. In their work the influence of Morris and Mackmurdo (the latter of the Century Guild) was to be clearly traced. The designs turned out

40

under these conditions caught the popular fancy and there is evidence, in their very success, that the public were about that time becoming very much more design conscious. But this awareness, because nurtured upon designs of strongly individual style, had a tendency to mistake mere stylism for true worth; and, too often, not only the manufacturers but the converters and the distributors found it profitable to establish and retain certain stylistic tendencies with which their names were identified. Throughout this transitional epoch Cummersdale never lent itself to pronouncedly stylized designs, although the freelance artist was frequently employed and always encouraged.

These changed conditions soon became well established and the Company, through their own organization, continued to work harmoniously with the free-lances, purchasing a variety of designs, many of which supplemented the ranges of the established merchants with world-wide distributory organizations.

We may here recall the names of some of the artists who contributed to throw lustre upon this period of transition, following in the wake of the distinguished example of William Morris. The best known to us were men like Walter Crane, Lewis F. Day, C. F. A. Voysey, Burns and, somewhat later, Sydney Haward, Rex Silver, Albert Griffiths, A. W. Mills Porter, J. Scarratt Rigby, J. M. Doran and many others, all of whom had their own style and specialities, ingrained by their individual temperaments.

Similarly the group of clever designers who followed on, such as P. Butterfield, H. C. Bareham, G. Willis, Edgar Miles and T. R. Carey, who by their work upheld the high standard set by their precursors, formed an important link between the merchant and the textile printer.

And so we come to the era of 'contemporary' design, represented by men of the younger school, with a flair for simplicity and a tendency to the abstract. By their special type of genius the best of these have created a revolutionary type of modern design which is, in many cases, well suited to the taste of the modern generation. Our experience is that some of the chief and notable exponents of design in this contemporary field are women, many of whom have established reputations entitling them to rank among the leading designers of textiles today.

During a period of over forty years' experience, meeting designers and discussing the merits of designs, many amusing and interesting memories might be recalled, almost invariably arising as the result of a clash between the personal 'vision' of the artist and the general recognition of what is and what is not a good design in relation to the technical problems of production.

In this field perhaps one of the most interesting personalities ever to be met with was that genius in 'oils', Louis Silas, who was especially active in the period between the two world wars. He was an amusing and lovable character, but a great headache to the producer who was confronted with the problem of transferring his designs from the paper to the cloth. All his work was done in oils on sheets of brown paper. His subjects were mostly of a floral nature and his great gifts with the brush enabled him to complete a design in an extremely short space of time.

To give some idea of the rapidity with which he was able to work, he produced for our approval one such floral piece in which we were very interested. We saw at once, however, that it would be impossible to transfer the design to the cloth by any normal process, since it was drawn without regard either to scale or size. Because of this, despite our interest, we were compelled to reject it. Within two days he returned with the identical design adapted to the scale we required, which meant that he had redesigned and repainted the whole thing.

Like many another artist, he was a little eccentric and always caused amusement among the staff by reason of a slight but fascinating impediment in his speech and a habit he had of continual movement, both of hands and feet, throughout a conversation. Nevertheless he had a charm of manner which endeared him to all with whom he came in contact.

CHAPTER FOUR

Some notable block-printed fabrics

PROBABLY ONE of the most fascinating aspects of the study of calico-printing is to follow the changes and developments which took place at the dictates of fashion and thus to note how both the designers and the craftsmen laid themselves out to meet the demands of an ever increasing *clientèle* both in the home and foreign markets.

There can be little doubt but that in the very early days before the coming of the railways, when the lumbering stage-coach and the local carriers' wagons were almost the only forms of transport apart from the primitive pack-mule, the distribution and sales were almost entirely local, although it is surprising how, at times, even in those days, commodities really in demand found their way to distant profitable markets. It was not, however, until the advent of the railroads and the commencement of what is now referred to as the Industrial Revolution that the demands of contemporary fashion and popular taste began to play an important part in the encouragement of economic development. A typical example of this phenomenon is to be found in the production of comparatively primitive and simple designs showing the unmistakable influence of the very beautiful and exclusive examples of painted, 'stained' and block-printed cottons and silks which, as already explained, found their way into the home market from the East. Because of their rarity and costliness, however, the latter were only to be found in the homes of the favoured few. The great less favoured majority, with that natural urge for emulation which is at the root of all fashion changes, were eager enough to brighten their homes by the employment of desirable substitutes once these English chintzes became available.

In all matters of following a fashion, set, as was this, by the 'upper ten', one usually buys, not so much what one would wish to have, as the nearest approach to it that is available at the time. And the gifted designer is one who can anticipate this wish by providing that availability should coincide with popular desire. It was in this direction that, at the time in question, the firm of Stead, McAlpin and Co. were able to consolidate their efforts and lay the foundations of that reputation which they have so jealously fostered in subsequent times.

The early fashions were confined to comparatively simple designs such as we have indicated and our first three illustrations in this series are devoted to examples which found favour among an ever increasing number of customers. In fig. 10 an early, English chintz obviously inspired by oriental specimens, we have a sober yet brilliant emulation of Indian *motifs* and the comparatively low-toned, rich colouring has been well matched by the English craftsman.

It was not long, however, before the designers began to introduce into their patterns more typically English *motifs*. Especially did they draw inspiration and instinctively create beauty from the old English country garden flowers beloved by all. Such homely types provided them with wonderful scope for developing a series of colour harmonies which resulted in a considerably wider range of effects than had hitherto been attempted in the home product. It is only in the textiles of this period that we find for the first time colour for its own sake playing the very important part which it has ever since displayed in English printed cottons. Figures 11, 12 and 13 show examples. In 11 we see a meandering composite of colourful floral sprays about a trellis, the whole against a faintly patterned ground. In 12, against a triple-leaf spotted natural cotton ground are set small floral sprays of roses, honeysuckle, poppies, lilac, etc., while in fig. 13, on a natural background is an intricate fretting of broken and cusped S-forms against which stand out small bunches of roses, in an all-over repeat. All three of these examples have the high gloss of the flint rocker.

A few words should perhaps be said here about these heavily

44

glazed chintzes in general. They were printed on a fine cotton cloth and the glaze gave a most effective lustre. It was originally obtained by the very primitive process known in those days as the 'Flint Block'. This was a fairly large lump of flint to which had been imparted a rounded, polished surface. Held in a casing of wood, it was suspended from above and worked on the rocker principle. The printed cloth was stretched upon the hard-topped tables and the flint was thrown backwards and forwards across the table. The constant friction of the flint gave to the cloth the necessary gloss. A flint-block is illustrated on fig. 14. The throwing of the flint was a task undoubtedly done by children, the motion being not unlike the throwing of the shuttle in weaving. As the demand for these glazed chintzes increased, and since the evils of child-labour were beginning to become a serious issue on the sociological side, it was not very long ere a mechanical method was devized to take the place of the old flint-block. Steam heat and friction were applied by means of a machine with steel rollers turning in opposition to a large revolving wooden bowl (see fig. 15).

Throughout the Victorian era, and in fact right through the nineteenth century, these chintzes were made so stiff and hard, with so brilliant a gloss that it is difficult to realize how the seamstresses of the time could ever have made them up into curtains and covers for furniture. Even more of a puzzle it is to understand how the women of the crinoline and other periods of voluminous skirts and 'tempestuous petticoats' ever found it possible to recline comfortably on chairs or sofas covered with these highly glazed materials.

In addition to an increased demand for these floral prints, for use as curtains and furniture coverings, there grew up, in the second quarter of the nineteenth century, a demand for printed fabrics which could be used for roller window blinds. The roller blind had 'come in' about 1825 and the fabric to be pulled up and down on the roller had to have special qualities. The Company realized the need and the great opportunity this new fashion provided. At once they rose to the occasion and began to put on the market various types of glazed chintz, which, as they foresaw, proved an excellent fabric for the roller-blind and, as events proved, shared its long popularity.

The types of design used for the roller-blind in the early phase of its long vogue were all printed by the hand-block method and it will be seen from the examples we illustrate that the stained-glass window and more or less gothic architectonic designs formed the basis for many. Our fig. 16, for example, block-printed in 1838, shows conclusively that the stained-glass window *motif* was by no means crude. Our figs. 17 and 18, while they adhere to prevailing 'gothic' fashion, can hardly have been so popular as the foregoing. In both we have the recurring architectural perspective, which abrogates the flat-surface insisted upon in one by the yellow stripes occupying the centre. The other example is made up by use of this same block in a more elaborate architectural framework.

Before very long it became evident that the truly extra-ordinary demand for the roller-blind prints could not be met by the slow hand-block printing method. So to cope with the increased orders the Company was among the earliest to produce a glazed chintz by the machine method from engraved copper rollers. It will be seen from the reproductions on figs. 19 and 20 that the result was all that could be wished. They give some idea of the variety of designs that were produced. These, of course, had to be limited to one or two colours which, at that time, was all the machines were capable of producing. But the firm's records show that various widths, between 30 inches and 60 inches, were printed—a necessary procedure since the roller-blind was being adopted generally and windows were obviously of varied pro-portions.

Another development which took place in this early period was what the contemporary records of the Company speak of as the 'border and filling', which became very popular for the embellishment of the 'four-poster' bed. There are many beauti-

46

ful examples of this type of floral chintz, all printed by hand-block and no account of the activities of the firm would be complete without putting on record at least a couple of specimens of these interesting and artistic productions. On fig. 21 we have an early example of 1837, in which the well printed and colourful floral sprays of roses and poppies reach the high-water mark of block-printing. The examples on fig. 22, with characteristic stiff glaze, is of about 1850.

The early Victorian period, so prolific of changes and marked by such rapid developments in the industrial field, culminated, one may say, in the Great Exhibitions of 1851 and 1862, the first 'British Industries Fairs' as they might well be called, in which all the chief artists, craftsmen and manufacturers were provided with a unique opportunity to show the world what Britain could contribute to the sum of world production. Among the multifarious exhibits gathered under the great glass roof in Hyde Park (the original Crystal Palace, later moved to Sydenham) none were perhaps more distinctive and interesting than those contributed by England's flourishing printed-textile industry. Already at that time it had gained an universal supremacy in the production and export of quality fabrics.

The Cummersdale Company, ably seconded by their artist-designers and skilled craftsmen, contributed to the 1862 exhibition a series of hand block-printed chintzes, which contemporary records tell us provided a magnificent display, whether considered from the point of view of design, execution or eye-captivating colour. As already recorded, they were awarded the gold medal for their class, an award which brought great rejoicing to the Directors and workpeople alike, not only because of the award itself, but because of the knowledge that the success was bound to bring in its train increased orders and, for the time being at least, assurance of full-time employment. The two principal designs which helped to secure this coveted distinction are reproduced in figs. 23 and 24. Both are very beautiful, the bold roses on a light ground in the one, the equally

47

striking groups of roses, poppies, etc., in the other being very fine. The latter is remarkable, too, as being of a soft, unglazed texture which must have lent itself admirably to curtain drapery.

These designs—the entire exhibit in fact—established the already high reputation they enjoyed in the intricate technique of multi-coloured printing and from that pitch of achievement the Company has never looked back.

Even before this triumph they had produced many memorable designs, some depicting notable or historic events. This type of design may perhaps best be exemplified by the very interesting and quaint topographical record of early railway history (fig. 25). It shows us a two-range repeat of vertically parallel views in which we see the primitive passenger coaches and transport wagons separated by vertical borders showing a coach and pair issuing from beneath an ornamental arch.

As the poles apart another famous chintz, produced at a somewhat later date, is one with a repeat of a floral bouquet, embodying the Rose and Thistle. This was especially designed to be used for the hangings and covers on the first royal yacht, the *Victoria and Albert*. If it is carefully examined it will be discovered to have incorporated in each repeat distinct and cleverly executed profile portrait silhouettes of the young Queen Victoria and her Consort, Prince Albert (see fig. 26). It is not known for certain just how these profiles came to be thus introduced, but tradition assures us that Her Majesty was fascinated by the design and that she herself pencilled into the tendrils of the roses the two portraits, which, of course, were allowed to remain. The story is credible, for it is well known that the Queen had considerable skill with her pencil. To this day these hidden profiles in the '*Victoria and Albert Chintz*' (as it is always called) are discovered with delight by all who examine this historic production.

There are many other printed fabrics on which historical events are commemorated. One we illustrate on fig. 27, showing the Coronation of Queen Victoria. It is a wonderful example of fine craftsmanship, both as regards the cutting of the blocks and the subsequent printing. This may be compared with the entirely modern example (fig. 28) which was produced in 1951 as a souvenir of the Festival of Britain. It is known as the 'London Toile' and is a fine 50-inch-wide engraved machine print. In striking contrast with the Victorian fabric, its finely engraved baroque medallions, enclosing views of the Tower of London, St. James's Palace, Trafalgar Square, the Boadicea group, Eros Fountain, etc., are linked by vertical bands decorated with floral sprays. The general effect is quite light and is printed on a correspondingly light ground.

But to return to block-printed fabrics, we may note, in contrast, that in the Victorian period many very simple designs found remarkable favour with the public and entirely justified the foresight of the Company in producing them in quantity. As an example, the ivy-leaf, for some unexplained reason, figured extensively in the decorative schemes in the home. Our illustration (fig. 29) shows an all-over ivy-leaf pattern with a pleasing hint of natural growth, which had, in addition, a border which gave it a bold effect for many decorative uses. No wonder this was popular. It is simple in concept and in colouring, suitable for either wide borders or hangings.

Less decorative, but of interest as evidence of royal patronage, was the series of monochrome block-prints made by Cummersdale for official use. This comprised a variety of 'badges', as we might call them, consisting of a number of more or less ornamental devices printed upon plain calico for use in the Royal Households. They are of quite considerable historic interest, their chief and possibly only use being to be cut out and sewn on dust-sheets to cover the furniture in the various royal homes. Some were small, some larger, according to their destined use. Fig. 30 has been selected as typical—a simple wreath with the name 'Windsor Castle' in the centre. The name was, of course, varied to apply to specific residences—'Royal Pavilion, Aldershot', 'Buckingham Palace', etc. When the Royal Family was not in residence, the priceless furniture, etc., would naturally be covered as a protection from dust and the sun. The block-printed devices must have been a very familiar feature to the household staffs (figs. 30 to 35).

This would seem an appropriate place to mention another Cummersdale production for official use which, however, was quite dissimilar in its nature. We illustrate (fig. 36) an indigo discharge square or handkerchief which was supplied to the Prison Authorities of Carlisle in the early nineteenth century. The example dates from 1840. It is not on record whether these handkerchiefs were destined for the use of the staff or the prisoners.

One of our great regrets, with regard to the designs of the nineteenth century, is that we are unable to couple with them the names of the designers. The era of the free-lance artist-designer had not arrived. But always Cummersdale's craftsmen designers were worthy of praise. In the early twentieth century, however, with the Company still producing beautiful examples of block-printing (both cottons and linens) one person stands out pre-eminently as calling for mention. His name was Harry Wearne.

Before the first World War he was associated with the well-known firm of J. Zuber and Co., in Alsace, who at that time held premier place on the Continent in the manufacture of wallpapers and printed fabrics. On the outbreak of war, when Alsace came under German control, he succeeded in reaching the United States of America. There he established himself in business as a converter, for the production of high-class printed furnishing fabrics.

He had a genius for design and colour and it soon became evident that his hand-block printed cottons and linens were destined to become best-sellers in the American market. In fact, during the five years he operated from his headquarters in New York he created a range of designs which should long be remembered in the history of the trade as one of the finest collections ever produced from one studio.

The whole of this range was actually made and printed at Cummersdale and it can truly be said that Wearne's success in the American market could never have been achieved without the able co-operation of the Cummersdale craftsmen. By their combined efforts in translating the creations of his genius into finished products a great dollar-earning market was established which became of material value to this country at a time when exports to the U.S.A. were so vitally necessary.

It is practically impossible within the scope of a book like the present to give any adequate idea of the extent and variety of these productions. But we have chosen half a dozen which will, it is hoped, give some impression of their importance. It may be said that they prove incontestably the potentialities of the genuine hand-block technique in the hands of a skilled and imaginative designer, seconded by craftsmen of ability and the resources of a factory such as Cummersdale.

The six selected examples are seen on figs. 37-42. In the order mentioned we have, firstly, that known as *Montague House*. It shows a very effective and beautiful design in full colour against a pale green ground, a design inspired by the masterpieces of the Dutch School of flower-painters. The design calls for twenty-six colours and seventy-six blocks were used in the printing.

Next we have a specimen showing the classic influence of the famous Italian Pergolesi, who, it will be remembered, worked in collaboration with the renowned Brothers Adam and contributed, with them, to the creation of a new decorative style. Charming as these two examples are, they have not the old-world appeal so clearly to be found in the *Old Chelsea* pattern. As its name implies, this design is inspired by the quaint beauty and universal popularity of old Chelsea porcelain. The colouring and typical hand-block 'feeling' of this fine example is obvious. Sixty-seven blocks were demanded to produce this charmingly decorative effect.

Perhaps the most famous and remarkable of all these hand-block printed productions comprising this collection is that known as *Old Vauxhall*. Based upon information contained in contemporary documents from about 1750 to the early nine-

51

teenth century, it recalls the fame and authentic social history of the famous Vauxhall Gardens, situated on the South Bank of the Thames. These famous gardens were, in their hey-day, a meeting place and promenade frequented by all the *élite* and celebrities of the age, including even members of the Royal Family. To get a true appreciation of this beautiful print, composite yet skilfully welded into an unified design, it should be looked at with the same minute attention to detail as would be devoted to, say, one of Hogarth's celebrated moralities. To add to its interest and contribute to its understanding, an outline 'key' has been prepared which gives the names of many of the famous people who Wearne has introduced into his composition. These include the Prince of Wales, afterwards George IV, Georgiana, Duchess of Devonshire, Hogarth the artist, Dr. Johnson the noted lexicographer, David Garrick the actor, Mrs. Siddons, premier actress of the day, and many others.

The fifth of this series is known as the *Clipper Ships* and is a most interesting and historical production, beautifully executed on eighty-four blocks. It proved of great popularity with the American public, since the 'clippers' represented were both American built. The interest centres upon these, two of America's most famous old trading ships, but, as a wood-block print, it has also its technical interest for us. One of the clippers is the *Belisarious*, which was built in Salem in 1794 for trade to the East. She carried sixteen guns and many were the valuable cargoes of tea, indigo, spice and so forth which she carried home before she was finally wrecked in the Bay of Tunis in the year 1810. The second ship was the *Flying Cloud*, built in East Boston in 1851. In her best days she created many records as a clipper, carrying tea from Canton to Boston. She met with an untimely end by fire in the harbour of St. John's, New Brunswick, in 1874.

We have left to the last of these six what is probably the most ambitious (as it was, too, the most costly) block-print design ever produced—the ever-famous *Tree of Life*. This design was undoubtedly inspired by the ancient traditional Tree of Life design so frequently the subject of those remarkable and beautiful *palempores* which were among the most renowned productions to be imported from India in the eighteenth century. But whereas the Indian cottons were often decorated with a combination of printing, dyeing and painting by hand, this Cummersdale production was entirely block-printed. No less than 390 blocks were employed and it took two years to complete. It was so designed that it could be produced as a panel with a border to a size of about nine feet by four feet six inches, or it could be printed as piece goods without the border or base.

During the many years that Wearne was active in New York his entire range was exclusively limited to the American market and it is only in recent years that this important collection has become available in the world's markets. Harry Wearne died in 1929. With his passing the industry lost a genius who, as so often happens in the case of truly great artists, can never be replaced.

With such proof as we have offered of the continued popular demand for hand block-printed textiles at home and overseas we need only record in conclusion that, in the period following the war, the hard glaze of which mention has been made was given up in favour of a much more pliable glaze, softer to handle and easier to make up. This softer effect appealed very strongly to the decorative specialists of America and resulted in very substantially increased orders for these beautiful 'Old English Chintzes'.

Unfortunately, however, the narrow twenty-four inch width, which had held sway for so long in the home market, as well as for export, was found to be unecomical for the requirements of the American clients, who were making much use of these materials for summer curtaining and other household draperies. So, to meet the demand (since 'the customer is always right') it was decided to discontinue the narrow width production in favour of the so-called 'double width' (i.e. the forty-eight to fifty inch).

This changeover was in some respects a comparatively simple

matter as the same blocks could be used with but little alteration. The only serious problem was provided by the printing tables. The narrow-width tables became obsolete and had to be replaced by the much wider tables demanded by the new widths. It was an expensive initial outlay, but one which proved amply justified by subsequent experience in the terms of increased demand. Why this practical change had not been instituted years before is one of the mysteries of the industry and serves to show how conservative our predecessors were, seldom making any alterations in their traditional methods until circumstances forced them to do so if they would keep abreast of the times.

To round off this review of the valuable heritage we have in this continued vogue of the 'Old English Chintz' we may here show the reader a series of examples depicting types of design used throughout the past century and a half. From a study of these it will be gathered that, in this long-lived type of printed furnishing fabrics, 'fashion' has changed but little. For the most part, based as they were upon nature's own gift of flowers and foliage, the chintzes have adhered faithfully to a persistent tradition based upon an inborn affection which will surely live for all time. They range from the comparatively simple, highly glazed floral sprays of the eighteen-twenties and thirties, reproducing in somewhat stylized fashion old English roses, fuschias, convolvulus, sweet-williams, etc., to the fine, full-coloured bouquets of the 'sixties' in all their bold, natural beauty. We may note, however, the fine 'old style' effect of fig. 46, almost Jacobean in feeling, of roses, campanulas, and exotic blooms on a brown ground of patterned silk effect. This is a block and machine combined technique. From this we may pass to the very pleasing thirty-inch all-over meander of roses, tulips, double poppies of about 1840 (fig. 49) and the very effective conception of exotic birds and flowers on rusticated stems, a stiffly glazed product of 1850 (fig. 54).

One of the most fascinating features of the nineteenth century chintzes was the demand for colour in the grounds, as a change from white or natural ground, so long the vogue. This demand

54

was met by the ingenious method of putting in what became known as a Stormont or stipple ground in pale tint, an effect obtained from a very fine pin spot engraved roller. Such rollers were at times engraved to give the effect of a small diaper, or curling pattern, others were plain pin spots giving the effect of a pale plain ground.

The technique employed in the inclusion of these Stormont grounds (also known in the industry as fancy grounds) was this. When the printing of the design had reached the 'finished' stage, blocks were made exactly to cover the shapes of the designs. These blocks were used to overprint the latter with a thick solution of paste which was then allowed to dry. The cloth was then put through the machine carrying the single roller patterned with the fancy ground which printed all over the design. The latter, being covered by the paste, resisted the colour. A subsequent washing process removed the paste and the result was that old-world effect which became so popular in certain markets.

It is believed that this process (or should we say this effect?) was employed, if not actually invented, by the craftsmen at Cummersdale in the very early part of the nineteenth century and in many designs its use is continued to this day. So far as is known, it was never practised by any other calico printers.

CHAPTER FIVE

Memorable machine-printed fabrics

SOMETHING HAS ALREADY been said of the advent and development of machine printing. As with many another important invention, it started in a small way, and although Thomas Bell invented the first rotary machine for engraved printing from metal rollers in 1783, it was some considerable time before any great development took place. Though actually in use by Livesey Hargreaves and Co. of Preston in 1785, half a century elapsed ere the first machine was introduced at Cummersdale by Thomas McAlpin.

These early machines were capable of printing only simple colour designs, chiefly of the type then used for roller blinds and piece goods in stripes and spots. But in early Victorian days designs were already being printed in polychrome. As yet, however, the machines could not compete, either in variety or beauty, with the hand-block printed fabrics.

During the mid-Victorian period, when the popularity of printed calicoes was greatly encouraged by the increased output by machine, a vogue arose for a revival of the earlier designs, to which reference has already been made. As a particular phase of this revival we must here mention an enterprise intimately associated with Cummersdale.

Oriental *motifs*, exotic birds and floral designs had held the market so long and were so identified with the hand-block process that the time seemed opportune to branch out in a new direction. So the Company turned its attention to the designs of C. P. Oberkampf who, in the mid-eighteenth century, had established a print works at Jouy and, by a method of engraving on copper plates, had created a wide demand for certain monochrome pictorial designs. These seemed to be suitable for reproduction by machine printing.

By this time Cummersdale had in their engraving shops some of the most skilful engravers in the industry, so they decided to reproduce a series of what had come to be known as 'Jouy designs'. In coming to this decision they well knew that there were difficulties to be overcome. Oberkampf had achieved his early success printing from copper plates on a flat-bed, although later he attempted to transfer his designs to rollers as he could not meet the demand he had created by the slow flat-bed process. It was therefore seen that, if Cummersdale wished to achieve its aim of putting on the modern market these old designs, they must first master the problem of reproducing this very fine quality of engraving on copper rollers. Fortunately such was the technical skill of their engravers that all difficulties were overcome and many of the Jouy designs when reproduced were acclaimed masterpieces by all in the industry. As examples of this technical triumph we illustrate (figs. 59 to 61) two or three designs which had a great and wide success. Fig. 59 may be taken as representative of the best period of Jouy design. It is composed of various 'Empire'-style *motifs* in red on a trellised natural ground. This is followed by a design based upon Pompeian *motifs* and, as a striking contrast, another fine design incorporating a blend of romance and sporting scenes in one repeating design.

In looking at these reproductions it must be borne in mind that the effect is produced on one roller only, all the shading being achieved by a series of graduated stipples which, by the engravers' skill are so minutely disposed that the finished product resembles and has all the charm of a seventeenth century dotted print. These productions definitely add another chapter to the long history of Cummersdale's achievements.

About the same period another revival was attempted in a similar class of fine engraving, only more colourful in design, inspiration for which was sought in the productions of the Spitalfields silks of the Huguenots and the printed fabrics of the so-called 'William and Mary' period. This resulted in numerous new creations of more colourful and bolder type of which the example shown in fig. 62 is perhaps representative. This particular pattern became known the world over as 'The William and Mary Basket'. The design was achieved by a dual process—a combination of block and machine printing. The outline and the parts in red were engraved-roller work, the remaining colours being added by hand-block printing.

It was not until after the Franco-Prussian War of 1870 that the by then greatly improved multi-coloured printing machines began to be regarded by the industry as being the valuable asset they subsequently proved to be.

But, ever abreast of the times, the Company at Cummersdale kept pace with this new development and upheld their reputation by commencing to install machines capable of printing in up to twelve colours in various widths. In taking this step they had the benefit of being able to take full advantage of the first-class methods and experience which had been employed in their engraving shops, by then second to none in the country. Coupled with this, the introduction, about the same time, of the improved coal-tar colours gave the Company the advantage of being able to put upon the market designs of a similar excellent standard to those previously printed by hand-block. These designs were selected carefully from the portfolios of the best artists of the day, not only in this country but also the studios of Paris, which by this time had begun to realize that there was a great future for the commercial designer on the textile side.

By reason of their enterprise and foresight Cummersdale soon became one of the most important producers of high-class machine-printed cottons and linens, in much the same way as, hitherto, it had enjoyed a world-wide reputation for its hand-block printed fabrics. In part this success was due, of course, to excellent production management, built up from generation to generation, which allowed these high-class machine-printed goods to be sold at a moderate price, well within the reach of the middle class public both at home and abroad.

There are some of us who can look back to the late Victorian era when, as in a golden age, commodities in general, including, of course, printed textiles, were almost given away in comparison with modern money standards. It was a period when domestic architects were introducing the casement and discarding the older sash window. This seemingly unconnected feature brought into being new designs for curtaining of bolder and more colourful styles.

And then, at the turn of the century, *L'art nouveau*, born, one may say, at the Paris Exhibition of 1900, came to give a still further directive in design and colour. After a short-lived spell of popularity, this gave way to less abnormal styles in which the influence of the 'Arts and Crafts' teachings of William Morris, Lewis Day, Voysey and others recovered their sway and paved the way for the gradual evolution of the quite distinctive designs in full colour which characterized the productions of the era between the two world wars.

During this decade of struggle for the revival of prosperity competition became very keen in the industry, British products having to vie with both their French and German competitors. Even more serious, perhaps, was the fact that America, who up to this time had been a constant and valued customer for British traditional machine-printed designs, began to develop her own textile industry, doubtless constrained to do so because of the cessation of supplies while the war lasted. It soon became evident that the great United States market could no longer be counted upon as England's best customer. A contributory factor was that the vast yardage she could count upon 'consuming' within her own borders enabled her to 'mass-produce' in such yardage volume that she was able to give her consumers what must have seemed 'cut-price' terms. Added to this, her tariff system made it very difficult for the British producer to compete with her price-levels even with a minimum of profit.

In spite of these competitive drawbacks, Cummersdale never deviated from its very earliest tradition of producing those fine and distinctive designs which past experience had taught them to be the best policy. They continued to act upon the conviction that, whether block or machine printed, a well-drawn design, artistically coloured and instinct with life, would always find a ready sale.

In many industries it is the popular belief that, if the aim is to be progressive, a producer must send out into the markets to discover what is wanted and only then proceed to fill the want. This was never the policy or belief of the calico-printer, particularly of Cummersdale, which has always proceeded upon the belief that taste and fashion, at least in furnishing and sartorial fabrics, are responsive to intelligent leadership. As far as taste is concerned, appreciation can only set its seal of approbation upon the finished product. The artistic merit and technical perfection of a design must be augmented by an imaginativeness which will compel approval. For taste—public taste—can ever be relied on to select the good from the less good, and prefer the best. This slight excursion into the psychology of fashion has been prompted by an urge to demonstrate that this belief has been the very foundation-stone upon which the progressive policy of the Company has been built. It is, perhaps, its greatest asset.

We must now draw the reader's attention to some of the most popular and successful designs that Cummersdale has produced for all the principal merchant converters in the section of multi-coloured, machine-printed fabrics.

The early designs for machine-printed materials, like most tentative or exploratory concepts, were of a comparatively simple nature, but in artistic qualities they were mature—and so an augury of success. Many early writers in speaking of the history of calico-printing deplored the advent of the new mechanical age, asserting that it would result in the destruction of all spontaneity and beauty. This view was never taken seriously by the production staff at Cummersdale and, in the active development of the mechanical technique the same amount of care and forethought was given to design and colouring for the machine as, in the old days, had been given to the block-printing method.

Proof of the wisdom of this policy can be seen in some of the very early thirty-inch machine chintzes which, before long, found favour with the public. This public was the larger, not only because the pricing was lower, but also because there was at the time an increased appreciation of artistic values, the result of the spread of education and the pride taken in the tasteful furnishing of the home by an ever growing section of the public. Probably one of the most important factors in bringing about this state of affairs was the method of advertising by the converters and distributors and the publication of magazines with their well-illustrated articles, the theme of which was the desirability of cultivating comfort and beauty in home adornment. Thus, encouraged by an intelligent and ever increasing demand, the producer was induced to keep up the standard which had in the first place enabled him to build up his reputation.

Figs. 63 and 64 represent examples of thirty-inch chintzes, but it must be remembered that they by no means exemplify the limits of the machines' capabilities. They do show, however, that the fears of many that the machine would destroy the artistic qualities of the products were without foundation. Products though they were of massive machines teeming with intricate technical devices, so widely differing from the intimate simplicity of the wood-block, the result in the hands of well versed craftsmen was a perfect triumph not only for the technicians but also for the skilful engravers of the rollers.

One of the striking examples of the latter's prowess, apart from the 'Jouy' copies previously described, is to be seen in our reproduction in fig. 65. The design is printed on a fine thirty-inch cotton. The engraving of the black outline roller was a masterpiece of precision and was indeed used as a decorative motif independent of the full-coloured design. The writer well remembers seeing it employed as a full-length wall-panel in the main entrance of one of New York's most important establishments in the interior decorating business. Its effect was most impressive.

Another fine example of a thirty-inch machine printed chintz can be seen in fig. 67. Known as the 'Chinese Lady', this boldly *chinoisserie* design with its reserved baroque panels on a deep red ground in which a Chinese lady with parrot and cage is seen seated beneath a small canopy, is a beautiful production made from a drawing by a well known French artist. The sales from its first printing were a great disappointment to its converter owner, although it was admired by many of the decorative artists of the day. Few, however, saw any practical future for it—until it was shown at one of the early British Industries Fairs, where it was shown as a quilted bed-head and bed-spread. It was there admired and chosen by a member of the Royal Family and from then on its success was assured, with the result that many tens of thousands of yards have been printed.

Another excellent testimony to the engraver's art at Cummersdale is to be seen in the 'Floral Vase and Swag' design, which is shown in fig. 66. It is confidently anticipated that it will have a long life and in time become an 'old master'.

For some decades now the popularity of the narrow, thirty-inch machine prints among the more commercial types of design has waned in favour of the broader, double width, better known as a fifty-inch, although it is well known that the narrower width is the more economical for the making up of loose covers, etc., for furniture. Most of the export markets favour the double width, however, and to meet this demand the Company has for some years produced a series of fifty-inch machine prints which have retained their standard of quality both as regards design and colouring.

Many of these have earned widespread popularity by virtue of their variety and beauty. The examples shown in fig. 68 and 69 will give some idea of their styles, ranging from 'Elizabethan' and 'Jacobean' to the 'Modern Floral', 'Contemporary' and popular 'Sampler' types. On figs. 70 to 75 we show, of these fifty-inch machine prints, an 'Old English Floral', of twelve colours on coarse linen; a 'Modern Floral', printed on a woven stripe ground; a 'Contemporary' printed in vat colours of stylized floral sprays, another with ivy-leaf *motif* on a ground of green and drab; a 'Floral Georgian' and a 'Sampler' in twelve colours, imitating the sampler of the early nineteenth century with its formal stitchery in coloured wools.

One of the great advantages of these present-day machine-printed fabrics is that they are all in fast colours. This fact has much increased their popularity—especially in tropical climates. Added to this it is safe to say that there are no more pleasing and economical productions suitable for all furnishing purposes in countries where heat and powerful sunlight have to be met with as a problem.

It would be impossible even to hint at the immense variety of designs produced in this machine range each year. But it can be stated that the number is well over a hundred, ranging from three or four coloured designs to the full-blooded twelve colours with all their additional effects produced by stipple and shading.

It might well be thought that a Company with the long traditional background of Cummersdale would not take kindly to contemporary design, such as that of the last twenty or thirty years with its geometric formalizations and abstract forms. But the present generation has found in this phase a type of decoration more to its taste, both as regards design and colour, than the traditional creations of their predecessors.

In the early stages of this change in taste, which none perhaps expected to have more than a short span of popularity, most of the designs were produced by the method of screen printing. This enabled the convertors to feel their way in the various markets without any great yardage commitments. But it soon became apparent that the demand could not be met from the screen production tables. It was not very long, therefore, before many of the more advanced types of contemporaries were being produced in volume yardage by the machine method, which had the advantage of reducing the production costs and bringing the finished products well within the means of many of the younger generation who were interested in the furnishing of new homes.

As frequently happens in any change of style, contemporary design, partly because of its novelty, very soon became a 'priority' in the yardage production schedule. As regards its popularity, however, one thing seems certain—that purely abstract designs, although they may fascinate by their colour schemes and arrangement, and have a definite appeal to the more advanced taste, do not find unqualified favour with the general public. One good reason for this is the psychological one that the human mind is, and always has been, so constituted that it only finds lasting satisfaction in the beauty and significance of Nature's own forms, and if any contemporary style of decoration is to live long and become popular it must be founded more or less closely upon Nature's own designs. This contention is ably supported by an examination of the products of Cummersdale. A careful analysis shows that the really successful designs of a modern type, such as those shown in figs. 76 and 77, all of which have earned reasonable patronage in many markets, are founded (even if somewhat remotely) upon Nature's forms.

CHAPTER SIX

A supplementary chapter of items of interest

AMONG THE ARCHIVES of Stead, McAlpin and Co. is an interesting Indenture, dating from 1843, i.e. from the early days of their activities at Cummersdale, which we are tempted to quote in full as it throws light upon the conditions obtaining a century and a quarter ago. It binds John Dixon, Junior, as an apprentice to the Company as a calico printer for the usual term of seven years.

THIS INDENTURE made the eighth day of February in the year of Our Lord one thousand eight hundred and forty three. Between Thomas McAlpin, Hugh McAlpin, John Stead and Duncan McAlpin, all of Cummersdale in the County of Cumberland, Calico Printers, of the one part and John Dixon Junior of Carlisle and John Dixon Senior his Father of Carlisle aforesaid Calico Printer (surety for the said John Dixon Junior) of the other part. Witnesseth that the said John Dixon by and with his own consent, freewill and good liking hath put, placed and bound himself Apprentice to the said Thomas McAlpin, Hugh McAlpin, John Stead and Duncan McAlpin to be taught and instructed in the said trade, business or occupation of a Calico Printer, which the said Thomas McAlpin, Hugh McAlpin, John Stead and Duncan McAlpin now use and follow, to serve them as an Apprentice for the term of seven years to be computed from the Eighth day of March one thousand eight hundred and forty one and fully to be complete and ended during all which said term the said John Dixon Senior doth covenant and promise to and with the said Thomas McAlpin, Hugh McAlpin, John Stead and Duncan McAlpin their Executors, Administrators and Assigns that the said John Dixon Junior shall and will faithfully serve, demean himself and be just and true to them the said Thomas McAlpin, Hugh McAlpin, John Stead and Duncan McAlpin, their Executors, Administrators and Assigns as his Masters and keep their secrets and every-when willingly obey all their lawful commands. He shall do no hurt or damage to his Masters in their goods, Estate or otherwise nor willingly suffer any to be done by others, but shall forthwith give notice thereof to his said Masters. He shall not embezzle or waste the goods of his said Masters nor lend them without their consent to any person or persons whom-soever. He shall not haunt or frequent playhouses, taverns or alehouses except it be about his Masters business there to be done. He shall not at any time day or night depart or absent himself from the service of his said Masters without their leave, but in all respects as a good and faithful Apprentice shall and will demean and behave himself to his said Masters and all theirs during the said Term. And for the considerations hereinbefore mentioned the said Thomas McAlpin, Hugh McAlpin, John Stead and Duncan McAlpin for themselves, their Executors and Administrators do hereby covenant promise and agree to and with the said John Dixon Junior and John Dixon Senior his Father their respective Executors and Administrators in manner following, that is to say, that the said Thomas McAlpin, Hugh McAlpin, John Stead and Duncan McAlpin according to the best of their power, skill and knowledge shall and will during the said Term teach and instruct the said John Dixon Junior or otherwise cause him to be well and sufficiently taught and instructed in the said Trade or Business or occupation of a Calico Printer. And also shall and will during the first four Years of the said Term pay unto the said John Dixon Junior Four Shillings per Week and for the last Three Years of the said Term Five Shillings per Week, week after week, for which the said John Dixon Junior shall print Five pieces of Six overs in one day or otherwise print any description of work which his said Masters may think proper to put him to. And lastly for the performance of the several and respective covenants and agreements hereinbefore contained on the part of the said Thomas McAlpin, Hugh McAlpin, John Stead and Duncan McAlpin and the said John Dixon Senior respectively to be done and performed in manner as aforesaid. They the said Parties do hereby bind themselves unto the other and to the respective Executors, Administrators and Assigns of the other in the penal sum of Thirty Pounds of Lawful Money of Great Britain firmly by these presents to be paid by the party failing to perform to the party performing the several covenants and agreements aforesaid. In Witness whereof the said Parties to these presents have hereunto set their Hands and Seals the day and year just above written.

Signed, sealed and delivered in the presence of	Thomas McAlpin Hugh McAlpin John Stead
James Brown Duncan McAlpin	John Dixon John Dixon Sen.

In perusing this document we shall notice that, in the case of John Dixon Junior the usual term of apprenticeship is made retrospective—the seven years to date from March 8th, 1841, although the Indenture was drawn up in February 1843. This suggests that a trial period of two years had been allowed to elapse, at least in his case, before any binding document was executed.

Another interesting point to be noticed is that John Dixon Senior is spoken of as a Calico Printer, from which we surely may deduce that he was already in the employ of the Company. Here, therefore, we have a definite example of a son following in his father's footsteps. In fact it would not be too much to assume that the father had been one of those who had migrated with the firm from Wigton eight years earlier.

We may also deduce from this document that, in these early days at Cummersdale, Thomas and Hugh McAlpin were the Principals, taking precedence over John Stead, while Duncan McAlpin was apparently quite a junior partner, only signing the document as a witness.

The 'do's and dont's' set forth so clearly show us how seriously the relationship between the masters and apprentice was taken and how salutary the old custom of apprenticeship was for all parties concerned. In those days it was doubtless found very necessary to prohibit the betrayal of trade 'secrets', the wastage of goods or the frequenting of playhouses, taverns and alehouses, for fear that the youthful learner of the trade should at the same time learn less worthy habits, while bound to the Company.

We are reminded, too, how different from now were money values of a century ago and realize that four or five shillings a week was an adequate reward while the apprentice was serving his time. The thirty pounds fine for default on either side was an additional inducement for the apprentice to apply himself diligently and in due course produce his 'Five pieces of six-overs in one day' or its equivalent, as a proof of his ability to 'earn his salt'.

Although bound strictly in respect of all important matters, the apprentices would seem to have found opportunities (as boys

69

will) for enlivening their years of tuition. One of Cummersdale's oldest employees recalls with great gusto a trick played upon an old Irish block-printer who used to come to work wearing clogs, though for comfort's sake he changed into an old pair of shoes before starting work. One evening, when knocking-off time came at 5.30 p.m., he sat down upon a stool and slipped his feet into his clogs as usual. Then, getting up off his seat, he nearly fell over as he tried to walk. The apprentices had put a four-inch nail through each clog, nailing them fast to the floor!

In the old days the boys looked after the midday meals of the older men, who brought all kinds of food to be cooked or heated up upon the large stove which warmed the shop. A prime favourite with the Cumberland men was 'Potato Pot' and there was one old hand who frequently found his way to the stove just as the boys were setting the crisp brown potatoes ready on a dish. The visitor would, without so much as a 'by your leave' lift a potato from the dish and eat it. One day the boys carefully removed most of the floury interior from one and substituted cayenne pepper before placing it in a prominent place on the dish. Along came the man as usual, picked up the potato and began munching it. It was not longe before he made a spluttering and hurried exit and, to the boys' satisfaction, he never again helped himself to his mate's potatoes.

Many are the stories told by old-timers, in which it is not difficult to trace the hand of the sporting apprentice. One of the elderly back-tenters, it is said, used to fancy himself as an expert on tea and boasted that he could name any brand as the tea-tasters do. So six cups were carefully brewed to test him and he named each one as he sampled it. Only after his pontifical pronouncement was he told that all six cups had been brewed from the same packet.

A more edifying story is told by another old employee who, during the time he worked in the garrets, had a new tierer sent to help him in the block-printing shop. He was starting a new job, so the tierer had to assist him in getting the requisite colours prepared. The colours had been brought to the top of the stairs by the colour-boy and the printer, standing at the head of his long table by the trolley, said to his new assistant, 'See that pot of green? Bring it here.' Obediently the boy brought a pot to the tub, but it was a pot of *red*.

'I told you to bring that pot of green,' he said, pointing to it so that there could be no mistake. A little while later he told the lad to get him a red sieve, but he brought him a *yellow* one. Loosing his patience, the printer exclaimed, 'Damit, boy, I told you a *red* sieve. Anyone would think you were colour-blind!' 'So I am,' the lad replied.

When next the foreman came round the man complained, 'You've sent me a fine example this time: that boy can't read and is colour-blind.' But when the foreman said he would get rid of him he would not hear of it.

'The boy's got to do something for a living. Give him a month's trial,' he suggested and, finding the lad knew his figures, he marked all the colour-pots, sieves, etc., with numbers and thereafter the boy never made a mistake, though the two worked together for over two years.

Many more stories could, of course, be told which would serve to show that the 'atmosphere' existing at Cummersdale was one of friendliness and good will born of a strong, almost family tradition. As in the case of the Cummersdale staff, so the employees at the London offices are shown by the records of the Company to have been not infrequently recruited almost as if by heredity. It was by no means uncommon for two or more generations of a family to work for the Company, giving long years of devoted service. And when once established they would seem, moreover, frequently to have spent their whole working lives in the service of the Company.

As a memorable example of long and efficient service we cannot refrain from mentioning the name of one man within our personal experience—that of William Dixon of the London office. Although we are assured that he is not a descendant of the

John Dixons mentioned in the Indenture of 1843, yet his own record is notable. He entered the service of the Company at the age of fourteen and rose to the position of chief warehouseman. He has already completed over fifty years in that capacity and is still on the active list of the staff.

His knowledge of the various designs produced and his memory for periods and vogues are phenomenal. His ability to recall at will the identifying numbers, dates of production, and other useful particulars of designs has become a legend in, and beyond, the Company's office. He is regarded as a veritable 'Bureau of Exchange' by the merchants and decorative designers of the Metropolis—by all, in fact, whose desire it may be to trace the identification or history of any unfamiliar design, a service which the organization readily places at the disposal of all. Like most old servants, his value to the Company is acknowledged to be less in what he now actually does than in what he knows.

In contrast, it has of course at times happened that those who come to the Company's employ on the manufacturing side have stayed but a short while, unable to make the grade set by Cummersdale's production standards. We are told of one journeyman printer who, upon being given a four-block print to do as his first job, immediately put three of the blocks under the table, remarking that *one* block was enough at his last shop and it would have to be enough here. Needless to say his stay was brief.

We have mentioned above one noteworthy member of the London staff. At Cummersdale the firm is fortunate in having an excellent team of Production Managers and Foreman, most of them having served the Company for many years and are devoted to maintaining the high standard of work which has always played such an important part in every development of the Cummersdale productions. They will go down in the annals of the Company as pioneers of progress under the *aegis* of 'Automation'.

The old-fashioned method of forcing the cast-iron cores into the copper rollers necessitated the combined efforts of six men working for nine hours to change a set of twelve rollers. The Machine-Room Foreman devised a method whereby the task could be accomplished in a third of the time by two men operating a hydraulic ram. In effect the idea is the use of three separate cones instead of one solid cast-iron core. By his method the task of taking the cylinders from the core is also simplified and, by reducing faults and waste, the production is improved, since these cones maintain an even pressure over the whole length of the roller, whereas before the quality of the impressions tended to vary near the extremities.

This invention and the improvements already referred to in the method of hand-block printing are only two of many ways in which Stead, McAlpin and Co. are keeping abreast of the times, thereby upholding the reputation which they have earned and consistently retained throughout their long history of over two centuries' duration.

In 1955 H.M. the Queen conferred the M.B.E. on the Company's Foreman Engraver for his engraving skill and over forty years' service to the Industry. This recognition of a craftsman's skill was not only valued by the Company but by all his associates.

While engaged upon this instructive task, surveying the products of the Stead, McAlpin Company, the results of which are now before the reader, we have naturally been prone to compare them in our minds with the more aristocratic textile fabrics of which printed calicoes were and always will be the friendly rivals. Brocaded silks, damasks, tapestries, loom embroideries, etc., have never been, nor ever will be, ousted from popularity as decorative furnishing fabrics. But printed textiles have very substantially supplemented them as we have seen by adding a wide range of fascinating alternatives giving other and quite distinctive effects. Their creators have never aimed at imitation.

Because of their very nature, however, printed textiles have considerably less chance of long life and survival than the decorative fabrics we have referred to. Being in substance simple calico weaves, not reinforced by any of the complicated additional structure which woven patterns possess as a technical necessity, printed fabrics are comparatively frail. Though quite durable, they must wear out more quickly, washing, ironing, etc., contributing to eventual decay. Moreover, in the days before the advent of vat-dyes, the more or less fugitive nature of most of the colours tended to shorten the period of their effective usefulness.

It is therefore a matter of no little satisfaction that it has proved possible, from the productions of one company, to gather so instructive and comprehensive a series as these we have reproduced. The earlier examples are veritable 'museum pieces', antiques in their own right, while many of the more modern examples may well prove to be antiques of the future. As a whole, including as they do specimens both ancient and modern, they form a very valuable record of printed cottons throughout the last two centuries. This volume is intended, therefore, to be a whole-hearted tribute, not only to the beautiful art of the cotton-printer, but also to the prowess of a company whose long history and high endeavour has had so much to do with the development of the great industry of printed textiles.

APPENDICES

CHRONOLOGY

1498   Calicut, on the coast of Malabar, visited by Vasco de Gama.

1592   An English privateer captures the *Madre de Dios* with a cargo of calicoes, lawns, quilts, etc.

1600   British East India Company is granted Charter.

1602   Dutch East India Company founded.

1631   East India Company opens a trading post at Madras.
Royal proclamation permitting import of Indian printed calicoes.
Calicoes first brought to England.

1664   French East India Company formed.
East India Company establishes trading settlement at Calicut.

1670   The secrets of the Indian technique became known in Europe in the 1670's.

1676   Approximate date of the establishment of the first English print-works.
William Sherwin granted a patent for producing broadcloth in the Indian manner.
The Dutch Loom introduced into England.

1683   Indian calicoes being made in special sizes for the European market.

1685   Revocation of the Edict of Nantes.

1690   Réné Grillet, a Frenchman, petitions for a patent to print calicoes.
Several print works are operating in Surrey at this date, including that at West Sheen (Richmond).

1700   Bromley by Bow already a calico printing centre before 1700.
Import of Indian Chintzes prohibited.

1702   Excise Duty of 2d. a yard imposed on English printed fabrics.

1714   Duty on English printed fabrics raised to 6d. a yard.

1719	The Silk weavers march to Westminster to protest against the wearing of English chintzes.
1720	Prohibition of English printed cottons.
1736	The Manchester Act, allowing the printing of cotton fabrics if they have a linen warp.
1738	Calico printing first practised in Scotland.
1740	Bromley Hall works (Poplar) first mentioned in the 1740's.
1745	Bonnie Prince Charlie comes over the Border. About this time Kenneth McAlpin settled in Wigton.
1746	Battle of Culloden. First textile printing works founded in Mulhausen (Alsace).
1752	Earliest documented use in British Isles of engraved copper plates, by F. Nixon and T. Thompson at Drumcondra (near Dublin).
1757	Francis Nixon at Phipp's Bridge (Merton) from 1757-1765.
1758	C. P. Oberkampf founded print works at Jouy.
1760	Earliest surviving example of an English printed fabric. Oberkampf prints his first piece.
1761	The calico-printing industry first established at Carlisle. Earliest reference to copper plate printing in Lancashire. Robert Jones at Old Ford works. Earliest surviving example of engraved copper printing.
1764	Hargreaves invents the Spinning Jenny.
1765	John Collins of Hertingfordbury (Herts).
1768	Two women fined £5 by the Lord Mayor for wearing chintz gowns.
1769	Richard Arkwright's spinning machine.
1770	Taylor and Walker use wooden cylinder machines.
1771	First cotton printing works at Glasgow.
1772	Print works at Church (near Accrington) established.
1774	Ban on English printed cottons lifted.
1779	Crompton's 'Mule' invented.

1780	Date of earliest block-print in the possession of Stead, McAlpin and Co.
	Old Ford factory closed down.
1782	Excise duty raised to 15%.
	Broad Oak Printworks founded.
1783	Thomas Bell invents rotary printing by engraved rollers.
1785	Cartwright invents the power loom
	Bell's invention used at works of Livesay, Hargreaves at Preston.
1789	John Nixon's Company at Phipp's Bridge (Merton) closed down.
1790	Bromwell and Irving at Spittal, Wigton.
1798	Thornliebank Works, near Glasgow, established.
1801	John Forster, a banker of Carlisle, built Cummersdale Print Works.
1817	Forster, James and Co. of Cummersdale close down.
1825	Opening of Stockton and Darlington Railway.
	About this date the roller-blind was introduced.
1829	Stephenson's 'Rocket'.
1831	Final repeal of prohibition of English printed fabrics.
1835	Thomas McAlpin acquires Cummersdale works, then ruinous.
1837	Accession of Queen Victoria.
1842	Railway facilities extended to Carlisle.
1951	Great Exhibition in Hyde Park.
1856	First coal-tar dye (mauve) made by W. H. Perkin.
	(From this date well into the 1870's, and even later, other colours were discovered.)
1862	Great International Exhibition. Stead, McAlpin awarded two Gold Medals for hand-block printed fabrics.
1868	Discovery of alizarin.
1870	William Morris at the zenith of his powers and popularity.
	The Franco-Prussian War, 1870-71.
1852	The Century Guild founded by Mackmurdo.

1883   The Arts and Crafts Exhibition Society inaugurated.
1893   Stead, McAlpin purchase the blocks, etc., of Bannister
        Hall.
1900   Paris Exhibition, vogue of 'L'Art Nouveau'.
        End of Victorian Era.
1913   Omega Workshops opened by Roger Fry.
                    War Period
1920   The late 1920's saw advent of Screen Printing.
1925   Paris Exhibition. A turning point in history of Textile
        design. Era of geometric formalization.
1930   In 1930's Cummersdale developed the Screen Printing
        technique.
                    War Period
1948   Manchester Cotton Board founded.
1949   Exhibition of Printed Furnishing Fabrics at Manchester.
        Arranged by Stead, McAlpin and Co.
1955   Exhibition at Cotton Board. English Chintz, assembled
        by the Victoria and Albert Museum at Manchester.

HISTORIC STYLES IN DECORATION

From the 17th Century to the present time

ENGLAND

Period	Style		Style
		17th Century	
Tudor		**ELIZABETH, 1558–1603**	Early Renaissance
		Secular Embroideries of poetic significance. The incorporation of the Broderer's Company.	
		Tapestries. Petit Point. Hardwich Hall and other stately homes.	
Jacobean		**JAMES I, 1603–1625**	
		CHARLES I, 1625–1649	
		Christopher Wren } 1632–1723 Grinling Gibbons }	
Stuart		**CHARLES II, 1660–1684**	
		Chinoiserie and Indiennerie. St. Paul's Cathedral. Fire of London, 1666. Printed and Painted Cotton imported from Dutch E. Indies. Mortlake Tapestry. Works by Peter de Marque.	
		JAMES II, 1685–1688	
Queen Anne		**WILLIAM & MARY, 1689–1702**	
		Jacobean (?) Bedhangings. Spitalfields Silks by Huguenots. Importation from Holland of Lacquer Furniture and Delft Porcelain in imitation of Chinese.	

FRANCE

A.D.		Style
1603	**HENRI II to HENRI IV**	*Renaissance*
	Henri II's Tomb in the Church of Saint-Denis, one of the chefs-d'œuvre of Renaissance Art.	
1623	**HENRI IV to LOUIS XIII**	
1643	**LOUIS XIV, 1643–1715**	*Louis XIV*
	Madame de Maintenon. Lace Designs in Brocade. Alencon Lace.	
1663	Berain. Boulle, Du Cerceau. Lepautre, Lebrun & Caffieri. Claude Gillot, Watteau. Gout Chinois commences, 1670. Pillement's Chinoiseries.	
1683	Revocation of Edit of Nantes, 1685. Weavers and other craftsmen expelled, some settling in England. Introduction of Wall Papers in square sheets, Dufourcoy, Paris, 1700.	
1703	**REGENCY till 1723**	

English Period	English Events	Date	French Events	French Style
	ANNE, 1702-1714 Chinese Wall Paperhangings. Vogue for collecting Blue and White Chinese Porcelain.		LOUIS XV, 1715-1774 Du Barry and Pompadour. The Porcelain of Sèvres. Rococo or Barocque. Philippe de la Salle, 1723-1803, at Lyons (Maison Pernon), 'Vernis Martin', 1730.	Rococo
Early Georgian	GEORGE I, 1714-1727 Wren Dies, 1723. GEORGE II, 1727-1760 English Lacquer.	1723 1743	First Lace Making Machine, 1768.	
Adam	GEORGE III, 1760-1783 Adam, Robert and James. Piranesi, d. 1778. Pergolesi.	DISCOVERY OF POMPEII		
Chippendale	Great English School of Cabinet Makers. Chippendale, 1764. Locke. Mainwaring. Sheraton. Hepplewhite.	1763	LOUIS XVI, 1774-1793 Ranson & Fay, ornamentalists. Percier, Fontaine, Fragonard. Oberkampf's Print Works at Jouy. Designs by J. B. Huet & Pierre Prud'hon, 1784.	Louis XVI
Georgian	Hargreave's Spinning Jenny. First Block Print, 1780, in possession of Stead, McAlpin. Invention of Printing on Calico by cylinders on rollers, Thomas Bell, 1783. Stead, McAlpin's Factory built, 1801. Madder Printing, Berry Yellow. English and French Paperhangings printed in lengths, in general use, 1811.	1783 1803	Revolution, 1792. Directoire First Consulate, 1799 NAPOLEON, 1804-1814	Premier Empire
19th Century Regency, 1783-1820		1823	Lyons looms still active making silks, etc., for the Imperial Palaces of Versailles and Fontainbleau. Waterloo.	
Late Georgian	GEORGE IV, 1820-1830 Brighton Pavilion built. WILLIAM IV, 1830-1837 Cotton Printing. Dr. Perkin's Aniline Mauve, 1857. Vergnin and Renard discover Aniline Red, 1859. Great Industrial Activity. Decadence of Home Arts.	1843	LOUIS PHILIPPE, 1830-1848	
Early Victorian	VICTORIA, 1837-1901 Great Exhibitions of 1851 & 1862. Some Characteristic productions in block printed floral Chintzes, 1814-39. William Morris, Crace, Decorator. Owen Jones 'Grammar of Ornament' published. The 'New Art' Movement.	1863 Present time	NAPOLEON III, 1852 Franco-German War, 1870. REPUBLIC, 1875 Paris Exposition, 1900. L'art Nouveau.	2nd Empire

ILLUSTRATIONS

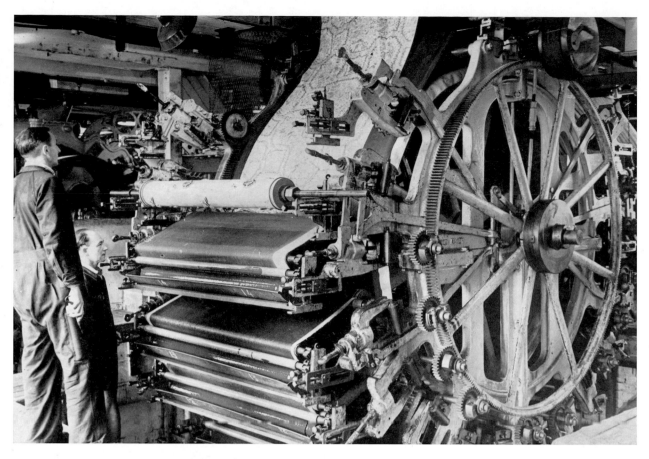

1. WOOD ROLLER MACHINE WHICH PRINTS UP TO 16 DIRECT COLOURS.

2. A BLOCKPRINTER AT WORK ON A CLASSICAL DESIGN 'CARLTON HOUSE', THIS CONTAINS 18 COLOURS AND REQUIRES 44 BLOCKS TO COMPLETE THE DESIGN.

3. SCREEN PRINTING SHOP SHOWING FULL LENGTH TABLES. THIS IS ONLY A SECTION, ITS FULL CAPACITY IS 11 FULL LENGTH TABLES.

4. IMPROVED MECHANICAL METHOD OF SCREEN PRINTING.

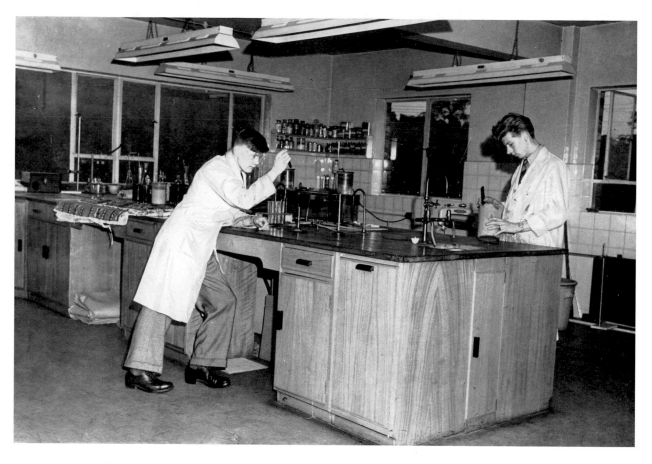

5. SECTION OF THE NEW LABORATORIES.

6. A BLOCK PRINTER AT WORK ON A TRADITIONAL OLD ENGLISH FLORAL CHINTZ USING THE NEW TIERER TRAY.

7. BLOCK PRINTER USING THE OLD TIERER TROLLEY (COMPARE WITH FIG. 6)

8. CORNER SECTION OF THE EXHIBITION HALL IN THE COTTON BOARDS COLOUR DESIGN AND STYLE CENTRE IN MANCHESTER.

9. FROM AN EXHIBITION OF FURNISHING FABRIC PRINTS FROM EARLY DAYS ARRANGED BY STEAD, MCALPIN & CO. AT THE INVITATION OF THE COTTON BOARD.

10. EARLY ENGLISH CHINTZ WITH ORIENTAL MOTIFS. 1838.

II. OLD ENGLISH GARDEN CHINTZ. 1839.

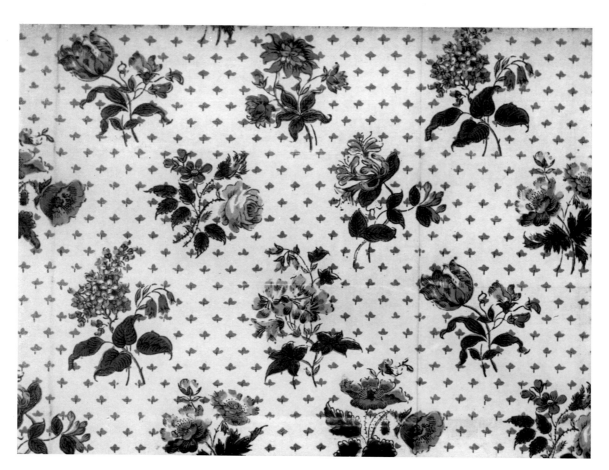

12. EARLY FLORAL SPRAY. 1840.

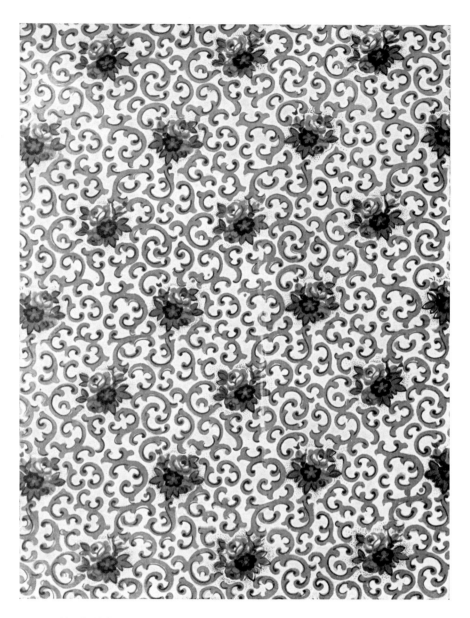

13. AN EARLY ENGLISH CHINTZ OF SMALL FLOWER POSIES ON
AN INTRICATE BROKEN SCROLL BACKGROUND. 1841.

14. FLINT BLOCK USED FOR GLAZING (TOP) SHOWS FACE OF THE
FLINT. (BELOW) SHOWS THE POSITION IN WHICH THE FLINT WAS
USED.

15. MODERN GLAZING MACHINE.

16. CHINTZ WINDOW BLIND. BLOCK PRINTED IN 1838.

17. GOTHIC WINDOW BLIND WITH STRIPE CENTRE AND BORDER. BLOCK PRINTED.
1840.

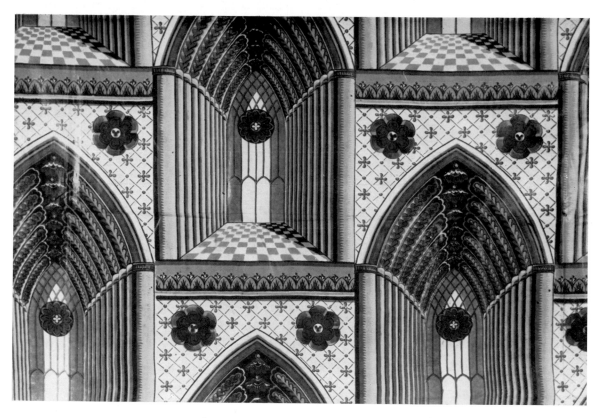

18. CHINTZ WINDOW BLIND. 1840.

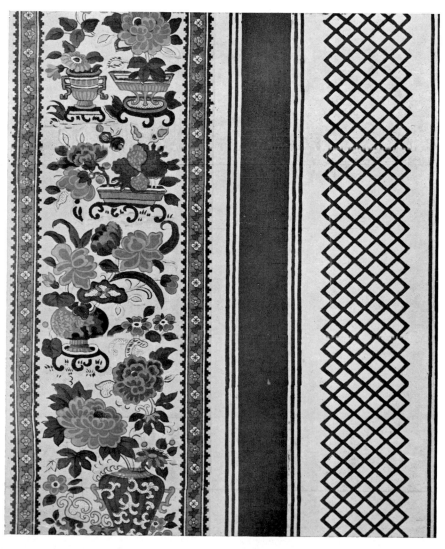

19. STRIPE AND BORDERED BLIND. 1845.

20. VENETIAN BLIND.

21. EARLY ENGLISH BLOCK PRINTED BORDER AND FILLING. 1837.

22. FLORAL BORDER AND FILLING 1850.

23. THIS FINE FLORAL CHINTZ WAS AWARDED THE GOLD
MEDAL AT THE GREAT INTERNATIONAL EXHIBITION OF
1862.

24. EARLY ENGLISH BLOCK PRINTED CHINTZ. 1840.

25. AN ENGLISH CHINTZ DEPICTING THE PRIMITIVE PASSENGER COACHES
AND TRANSPORT WAGONS. BLOCK PRINTED.

26. THE 'VICTORIA & ALBERT' CHINTZ. HAND BLOCK. 1850.

27 HAND BLOCK PRINT DEPICTING THE CORONATION OF QUEEN VICTORIA. 1837.

28. 'LONDON TOILE' A FINE ENGRAVING PRODUCED AS A SOUVENIR OF THE FESTIVAL OF
BRITAIN IN 1951.

29. 'IVY LEAF' BLOCK PRINT DATED 1852. WHITE GROUND WITH THREE
SHADES OF GREEN LEAVES.

30. WINDSOR CASTLE' HAND PRINTED ON COTTON. EARLY 19TH CENTURY.

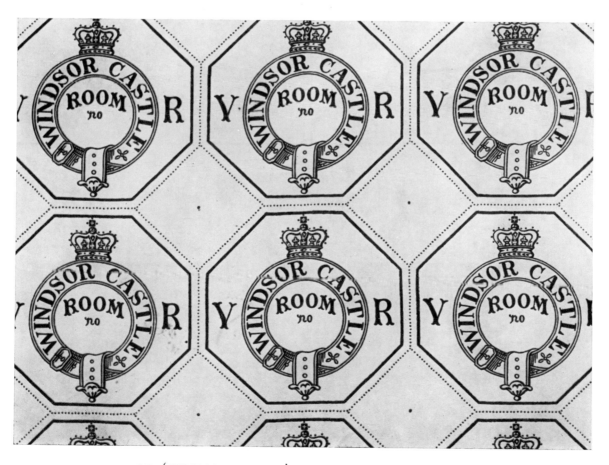

31. 'WINDSOR CASTLE' BLOCK PRINT ON COTTON.

32. 'ALDERSHOT PAVILION' HAND PRINTED ON COTTON.

33. 'BUCKINGHAM PALACE' HAND PRINTED ON COTTON.

34. HAND PRINTED ON COTTON.

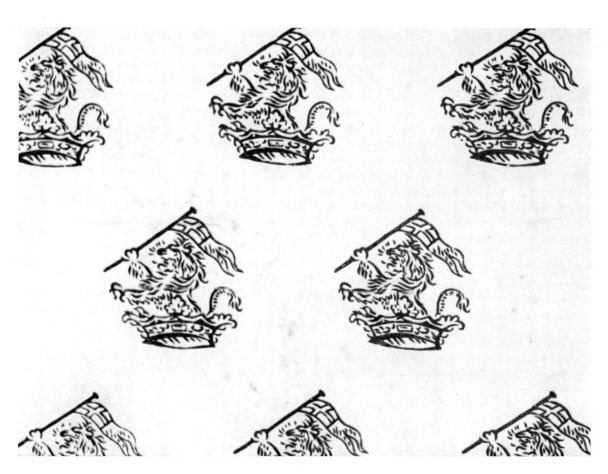

35. HAND PRINTED ON COTTON.

36. INDIGO DISCHARGE SQUARE OR HANDKERCHIEF.

37. 'MONTAGUE HOUSE' BLOCK PRINTED.

38. 'PERGOLESI MEDALLION' BLOCK PRINTED.

39. 'OLD CHELSEA' BLOCK PRINTED.

1. Hogarth.
2. Mme. Weischel.
3. C.I. Fox.
4. Georgiana, D, of Devonshire.
5. The Prince of Wales.
6. Mrs Robinson (Perdita).
7. Mrs Cornelys.
8. A Macaroni.

9. Mr Simpson.
10. Mrs Siddons.
11. David Garrick.
12. Angl. Kaufmann.
13. Sir Josh; Reynolds.
14. T, Gainsborough.
15. Mme, Saqui.
16. George Robinson.

17. Harry Vane.
18. Horace Walpole.
19. Miss Ashe.
20. Lady Petersham.
21. Miss Gunning.
22. Earl of Orford.
23. Old Q.
24. Capt: Topham.

25. Fanny Burney.
26. "Betty".
27. Boswell.
28. Mrs Thrale.
29. Dr Johnson.
30. Oliver Goldsmith.
31. Gibbon.
32. Smollett.
33. Burke.
34. Statue of Handel.

40. KEY TO 'OLD VAUXHALL'.

41. 'OLD VAUXHALL' BLOCK PRINTED.

42. 'CLIPPER SHIPS' BLOCK PRINTED.

43. 'TREE OF LIFE' BLOCK PRINTED. PRINTED WITH BORDER
TO FORM A PANEL.

44. BLOCK PRINTED FROM AN EARLY WIGTON COLLECTION. C. 1820.

45. HAND BLOCK PRINTED. C. 1820.

46. COMBINATION BLOCK AND MACHINE. A FINE EXAMPLE OF THIS EARLY
COMBINED METHOD. WITH ENGRAVED MOIRE EFFECT GROUND. C. 1825.

47. EARLY BLOCK PRINT. C. 1830.

48. EARLY BLOCK PRINT. C. 1835.

49. EARLY BLOCK PRINT. C. 1840.

50. EARLY BLOCK PRINT. 1845.

51. BLOCK PRINTED. 1847.

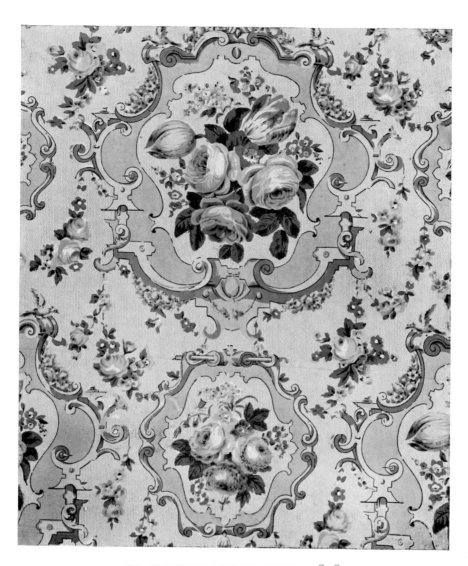

52. HAND BLOCK PRINTED. 1848.

53. HAND BLOCK CHINTZ PICTURING SYMBOLIC FLOWERS OF BRITAIN. LEFT HAND CORNER WITH THE ROYAL ARMS, THE CENTRE MOTIF CONTAINING THE PRINCE OF WALES' FEATHERS. C. 1850.

54. BLOCK PRINT. C. 1850.

55. EARLY VICTORIAN BLOCK PRINT.

56. HAND BLOCK PRINT 1840.

57. 'MAGNOLIA SPRAY' BLOCK PRINT. C. 1865.

58. MID-VICTORIAN FLORAL SHOWING THE BROAD STRIPE WHICH WAS THE FASHION OF THE DAY. C. 1870.

59. THE 'GOLDEN AGE' AN ENGRAVED REPRODUCTION OF AN EARLY 'JOUY'.

60. ENGRAVED REPRODUCTION OF AN EARLY 'JOUY'.

61. REPRODUCTION 'JOUY'.

By courtesy of Ramm, Son & Crocker Ltd.

62. 'WILLIAM AND MARY BASKET'. REPRODUCTION BY BLOCK AND MACHINE.

63. A CLASSICAL EXAMPLE OF A 30 INCH MACHINE CHINTZ.

64. A 30 INCH MACHINE CHINTZ.

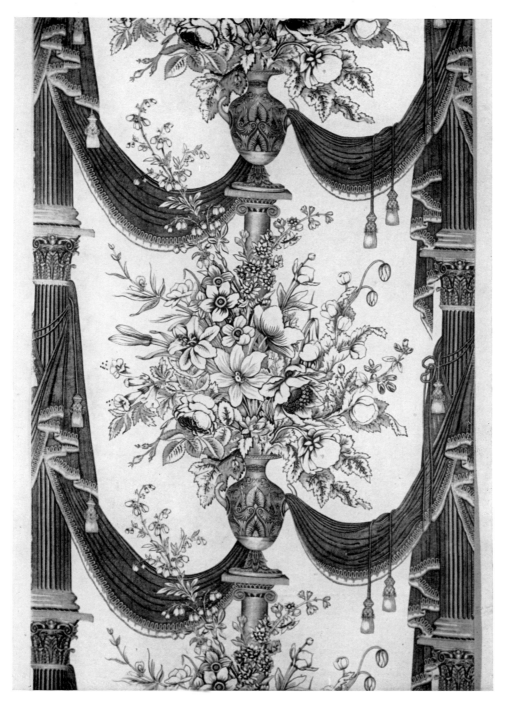

65. A 30 INCH MACHINE CHINTZ. PRINTED FROM ONE ROLLER AND FORMS
THE OUTLINE TO FIGURE 66 AND IS A FINE EXAMPLE OF THE
ENGRAVERS ART.

66. 30 INCH MACHINE CHINTZ. THIS IS FROM FIGURE 65 WITH ITS FULL
TWELVE COLOURS ADDED.

67. 'CHINESE LADY'. A 30 INCH MACHINE CHINTZ.
By courtesy of Walter F. Tranklin Ltd.

68. 50 INCH TWELVE COLOUR MACHINE PRINT. ELIZABETHAN EMBROIDERY DESIGN
PRINTED ON LINEN.

69. 'MODERN FLORAL' A TWELVE COLOUR 50 INCH MACHINE CHINTZ.

70. 50 INCH TWELVE COLOUR MACHINE PRINT. A FINE EXAMPLE OF A FLORAL BOUQUET.

71. 50 INCH TWELVE COLOUR MACHINE PRINT. REPRODUCED FROM AN OLD ENGLISH
FLORAL CHINTZ. PRINTED ON COURSE LINEN.

72. TWELVE COLOUR MACHINE PRINT.

73. 50 INCH TWELVE COLOUR MACHINE PRINT.

74. A SIXTEEN COLOUR SURFACE MACHINE PRINT OF FLORAL BOUQUETS ON LINEN.
By courtesy of Warner and Sons Ltd.

75. 'SAMPLER' A TWELVE COLOUR MACHINE PRINT.

76. 50 INCH MACHINE PRINT. CONTEMPORARY STYLE.

77. 50 INCH MACHINE PRINT. CONTEMPORARY STYLE.